Middle Earth Medicine

www.middleearthmedicine.com

First Published by Caroline Carey 2020

Photography: Ben Cole

Cover Design: Leigh Goodman

Artist: Brenda May

Typesetting and Layout: Eddie Sturgeon
Printed Word Publishing (part of the Scantech Group)

ISBN 9798631564480

Independently Printed

Middle Earth Wisdom

from Innocence to Sovereignty

by

Caroline Carey

Acknowledgements

I am grateful to Ben Cole, for the creative process and the support, for his wisdom in the embodiment of each of these archetypes and for bringing these resources together, to all he brings to this world of creativity, his talents his wisdom and his love.

To Helen Poyner, for midwifing me from one world to the next, with my feet firmly on the ground.

Thank you to Catherine Henderson for her editing skills, and her many hours of support and encouragement. For the laughter as we meander through the grammar and poetry, of a not so academic mind.

To Elixxchel Lily and Elisabeth Shrag, Dreamweavers of the Middle Earth Medicine Ways, for fully acknowledging the significance of this work and for dreaming with me its possibilities.

Gratitude to Rebecca Colby, for giving me the guidance, to restructure and align my body of work with my writing. For being so insightful into what I needed to create.

Gratitude to Kay Sexton, for keeping me on track with my spiritual principles, to ensure that I am inline with what is true and what is real. Thank you for the encouragement and for seeing the differences, so that I can get to know myself as a writer.

Thank you to my Grandchildren and their parents, their aunties and uncles. Becoming an elder is also part of being a granny, and you show me how to do it with grace, as well as fun!

The book Middle Earth Wisdom is a journey through the work of Middle Earth Medicine Ways, which is an inspiring art form, a journey to discover our own mythological stories and archetypes, the stories that are connected to old myths that live on in our own lives. We work with tools to develop and strengthen our emotional intelligence and a map for soul retrieval and healing. It is a place where we can do our inner-work in a creative way with tools to help us honour what has come before us, from the paths and tales of our ancestors, our culture and our heritage. A way to engage with our stories and discover what matters most from our own lineage of people.

The work that we follow on this Middle Earth Medicine journey, is greatly supportive to those creatives who are inspired and successful in their art, inspiring a better understanding of their own art's sacred journey. As well as those who may have become lost in their ability to express themselves, to find the resource of inspiration. Those who have entered too many times into a darkened place of despair. Those who long to shine yet have no or little idea of how to bring their light into the world.

The journey from innocence to sovereignty is at the root of this offering, to help heal that broken innocence, to begin to bring home the light of the soul, to embody our true purpose and reclaim the Sovereign of our birthright. That Sovereign, which is our own mythlogical and poetic identity, our true archetype and reason for being here.

Asking the question, 'Who am I?' lingers in the one who longs to know.

Maybe you are one of those who asks that question?

And here you just might find out... For this is soul-retrieval for our times in this world

For the dancers, the freedom makers,
the liberators of soul,
the poets and celebrators,
the magicians of our fold.

Contents

Preface

Our Cultural Wound

Some of our cultures have lost their connection to the sacred and the true meaning of it. What is the spiritual quest that our lives need to be devoted to when we are ready?

We each need to know our personal myth through the story of our life. The task is to reveal to ourselves what this archetypal myth is. We seek it from the unconscious and from the instinctual, to then find out how to enact this consciously into the world. It is from our life story that we will discover this, if we are willing to look deeply enough and uncover what lies hidden from view.

And we must find it within ourselves first, to then know what its purpose is and how useful it might be for others.

There is a world in pain, it calls us to deepen our searching and the exploration of our inner life and mystery. It asks us to do our own work, to heal what has been broken and to bring ourselves and our lives more into balance.

When we become aware that something is missing, is it not our duty to discover what that is and to call back into alignment the very thing that would make us whole?

When life brings about helplessness, and we are unaccomplished and unfulfilled, then we suffer along with our fellow men and women.

By lessening the agony, we can take stock and turn the light towards the dark and shadow, and determined we begin to explore that darkness, usually with a helping hand, because this work done alone is frightening, isolating and can turn us against ourselves if we are not careful. And so we come back to our grace and serenity, where we then become the example and inspiration for others to gain hope from.

This is a quest we must all make at some point in our lives.

To find the sacred marriage within us of the soul and the ego, of the feminine and the masculine, of the dark and the light.

The loss of this particular sacred quest that includes our Rites Of Passage, is held as a cultural wound in our society. How might we reclaim that quest?

For me, the reclaiming happens within and around our reconnection to creativity, to the soul, to a power greater than ourselves and by 're-membering' our broken innocence. The process of soul retrieval begins to help us reveal the myth of our identity and how we can begin to discover its archetypal energy and purpose.

We each have our own journey to enable us to discover this, and for me, I began to find it through my dance, my acting and my writing.

So Middle Earth Medicine is the journey to help us find that myth, that archetype, that story – helping us to find out who we really are and to create the rites of passage that our soul needs for community and individual healing.

* * *

We are healing this cultural wound, both collectively and individually, but when I look at the dysfunctions around me, I get a glimpse of the importance of this work, of why I need to follow this path and why I feel the passion that I do around it. We can do our healing by exploring our own myth, unveiling its story through our own lives and being witness to both its creative and dark sides of its character.

I lean towards the witches, the wise women and their craft, the medicine people of this land, the healing that happens via story-telling and poetry. The way one story can touch another and why we must speak the truth about our experiences.

So I feel that I 'fit' quite readily with the path of the sacred and the mysticism of life, it's what draws me into my own seeking path. I know its shadow too, the loneliness, the isolation and the inability to 'fit' into the ways of some of this more modern world.

At one time I leaned towards female goddesses, to the energy that I felt around me, to the worship of the moon and stars and what I could feel and sense and touch. What I could see and smell, what felt more real to me. I felt myself returning to old ways, to honour my story-telling, my imagination and my dreams. And I have always believed in my own God/Spirit, the way I choose to see this and believe in it, which is totally personal to me.

This belief has been with me all my life, since being brought up in a family devoted to the Church, to prayer and Christianity, but it soon became 'not my way' and I found my own way to honour my God/Spirit. I could feel that power all around me, in the atmosphere and in the natural forces. When I prayed, it was to that same God/Spirit, and I knew I would never let it go, because here was my truest friend and companion. And from there my true myth began to develop.

No, for me God was not a man sitting on a cloud looking over me, one that I should fear; but a kindness, a love so great it wrapped me in golden light and moved my body to that one great dance, that one rhythm that would turn my expression to tears, to an open heart and to laughter.

This in turn led to shamanism, because for me it felt all encompassing. For me shamanism includes all things; spirits seen and unseen, the elements and connection to nature. It is everything without dogma, without enforcing a belief on its followers. It met me just where I was, a God/Spirit that knew me, that wanted me to be happy, that wanted me to be real in the world, that wanted me to explore and to grow.

My continual trust stayed with a power greater than myself, where I knew there was always outside support.

Sometimes I notice where that belief has been left behind, simply because I have lost my way, or because I have tried to control or change something beyond my own power. I have forgotten my 'right size' in matters. It is not for me to play God, to know what is right for others. This has to be a constant reminder, particularly in the work I do. I have no idea what is right for another human being, but I can share my own story and hope to inspire.

Being brought up in a very religious way, always with prayer, is something I am eternally grateful for. Not because it was a path that I followed, but because it taught me the power of prayer. It taught me what happened when the community came together and prayed and sang or danced as one. I believed in community, a common-unity between like-minded people who wish to grow and learn. And from that kind of belief, I began to recognise and sculpt my own way and what worked for me. I found my own spirituality and learnt to trust that and be happy with that way. No longer that biblical male God but a presence I fully trusted in and found solace in.

I never felt alone.

I know that every land has its own descriptions of medicine and healing, alongside its traditional ways, but I learnt I can only follow my own.

Always exploring spiritual belief systems and ways of prayer, I thought that it would be good to explore other cultures' shamanism and indigenous wisdom, as so many of my friends and colleagues were. But something didn't sit well with me. I was fascinated with Siberian shamanism and some of the Scandinavian stories and myths I read. I understood that here lay the origins of shamanism. These myths and stories conjured up images that were very familiar to me, something that felt to be deeply connected to my ancestral lineage; the shape shifting and the knowledge behind many mythological stories and archetypes.

I took an interest in plant medicines from other cultures and lands that became known to me and I dabbled a little, experimenting with a few and seeing if that might be a 'calling' for me, ever wanting to find a root to my own shamanic path. I took part in ceremonies, drank of the medicines and felt into their effects, short and long term deciding then that that wasn't for me. It wasn't my medicine, it wasn't connected to my culture and I recognised that I did not need mind altering substances. Ecstatic dance gave me all I needed on that level.

I travelled to African lands and danced with the Bushmen doctors, engaging in their medicine dances, which I find deeply profound to this day and still engage in this calling as it transmits deeply into my own dance.

However, in the hunt for my own myth and soul's offering, my own connection to the sacred teachings and medicine of my own lineage, I did not look as deeply as I could have. And what was staring at me, fully in the face, was the indigenous belief and medicine of my own land, my own Middle Earth. This was the story of my own culture and what had been lost right here on these isles. Somewhere I embodied this but had never quite grasped it. I was under its influence very deeply and it clearly wanted to sing and dance through me. Its old ways have been lost, as invading cultures wiped out our own ancestral poetic nature and wisdom. Thus, we have found ourselves needing to harness other cultures' ways and bring them home to make them ours.

I related to this part of my journey from many angles and

felt it deeply in my bones; the old ways, the medicine of the hedgerows and meadows; the dance, the poetry, the ways of speech and verse; the birthing of babies and the holding of others in their deepest pain. The story-telling that takes us into the hearts and lives of others and helps us to recognise our own dreaming cycles.

In the '80s I became an herbalist, selling my wares through local shops and market stalls, people coming to my house to purchase bags of herbal concoctions and lotions and creams that I made on my stove. I took a diploma in herbal medicine and used this for a time as my medicinal offering, until my babies got a bit too big for me to be able to manage filling pots and making herbal mixtures. And so my children took centre stage and my herbal business was put into the background for a while.

Still there was more for me to do and understand. Writing has been one of my main mediums; it has helped me to unravel the story, and find a way to share with my communities, the wisdom that has seeped into the words I write. For writing and being creative opens up a channel for me, that comes from the feelings of the heart, from the flow of sensations that are created when paper and pen come together. This channel allows me to write down the tales being told; to tell my story, to find familiarity with others and to be a Seer of the truth.

Exploring my own myth was helped greatly by a particular theatre director I was working with at one time in my life, who helped me to discover one of the myths of my own story.

What story was I most fascinated with?

This supported my own growth in a very creative way and taught me how to support others to find theirs.

Can you adopt a child like curiosity and be fascinated with the fairy tales and myths that captured your imagination?

Middle Earth's Wisdom

In this Middle Earth offering we explore our purpose, our vocation and what some of us might call our sacred contract.

It is from this place, knowing at a deep core level, that the sacredness of spirit is at work.

It is a call of the soul where I myself have learnt to relax and trust the stages of my own life, of the deep mystery, and to begin dreaming in the next offering of my writing and teaching. As in all things, it is the dream or the imagining that first creates our journey. Then we learn to bring it into manifestation, one step at a time.

At first, I must become aware of my own Seer, the one that can oversee my life, witnessing the journey and what needs to be fulfilled along the way. Observing my own territory and inviting in the guidance that is needed, I must know who I am and where I am heading.

I learn that my work is to hold a level of safety and inspiration for others, to create a place where together we can discover what is needed for us and receive simple maps to support us. I encourage autonomy, with guidance in the dance and meditations, simply asking, 'What is needed here?' For we are on that journey from innocence to sovereignty, to reclaim what is rightfully ours and the power of our own destiny, that which is and always has been intended for us.

Sometimes my writing is poetic in its fashion, as words and meanings filter through the journey, even now, to reclaim those parts of myself that understand myself to be a writer and a poet, a Seer, a wordsmith, a truth teller, within this spirit-body and this world of matter.

That is my medicine, to find its myth and the language of it in these realms, an old forgotten language that I know can only come through my own way of speaking and the connection I have to my own bones, the bones of my body, of the one who dreams in her aspiration and calling, getting to know it with each step that is taken.

Always remembering that God/Spirit may speak in riddles and prose, in poetry and in sound, in the sharing with another human. And it is up to me to interpret it in a way that serves mine and others' highest good within this community of seekers.

We are dreaming in the lost words, the prose and the much deeper meanings that come from a second awareness that is not of the ordinary and mundane but of the 'other worldly' nature that this book's offering will explore and hopefully you will experience.

For me this is the language of the poet, the singer, the artist and the sensitive soul that life can overwhelm. The one that cannot quite make head nor tail of the goings-on of the world of man, that holds the melancholic spirit deep in the veins and knows trauma inflicted in the cuts that it finds hard to heal. The one who can become so lost with inner-turmoil that he or she is forgotten on the streets, left to consume more of the horror that has grabbed his or her arm.

Yes, this is for you my brothers and sisters. This is for you.

Notes

The Wheel of Soul's Return

Our life, full of experiences, gives us the opportunity to discover our own unique offerings and possibilities. Our birthings, our new beginnings, or the start of a project, we begin to dream with its possibility. We learn to accept the call as Spirit sent, where our soul is designing its own sacred contract and is connected from pre-birth in the realm of its dreaming.

We then take a journey around the Wheel to the Innocent stage where the imagination begins to vision in, with curiosity, what is possible to create from that contract, from our life story? What is possible from our awakenings and even sometimes from our challenges and wounds?

We journey from Innocent to Rebel, where we let go of old structures and immerse ourselves in the wildness of the Untamed Forest to release ourselves and explore the true nature of who we are. That mythological identity begins to show itself at this stage, take a look be curious, what do you see or remember?

This leads us to become the Apprentice of our own story and the manifestation of our own particular vocation, whatever that might be. Whether it is a particular project, body of work or even relationship. Being helped and guided by the understanding of our own repetitive patterns, by allies and guardians. We form together that story, we start to see more clearly that archetype, as each story fits with an old, old tale that we may have read in a fairy tale as children.

What did we draw, what did we paint, what dances did we dance?

The Wheel continues to be our guide, through adulthood with the Artisan and the Thespian, creating and acting from that place of creativity. Parenting the qualities we aspire to as individuals, showing our art to the world and manifesting change and fruition.

Knowing and maturing our purpose, we become the Sovereign and Archetype of our own Majestic garden, stepping into the responsibility needed for the task set out to us and those we must serve.

Accepting the humility of our own Sacred Fool, that we might relinquish the hold that our ego has over us. Trusting in a power greater than ourselves, the Sacred Fool reminds us of who we really are, how to find humour in our story and our humanness.

We must now awaken fully!

Leaving no stone unturned, we aspire to be the Wise Elder of our own making. Standing, staff in hand with that Sovereign vibration and the embodied calling that is here to serve. Surrendered in acceptance of who we are, we know ourselves and are able to honour our ego as the hands of the soul.

Now, as that Wise Elder, we are here to serve the Innocent's dream and whatever needs our support, bringing it into new life...

And the Wheel turns again...

* * *

Exploring our purpose or vocation means accepting all our experiences and unraveling some of those life long stories we have held, sometimes in the dark or run away for fear of opening up the wound too fully and the break down we suspect may happen, yet those very wounds control and rule our lives in ways we may never have realised.

Our purpose is born and sculpted through us, and the challenges we meet along the way are divinely there to grow this. To shape us into who we are, to reveal that archetype and what we are here to be in service to. Yet how we view our own stories might need to make way for something entirely new. Something even more revealing and much more in line with our potential.

This Middle Earth Wisdom book takes us through the work of Middle Earth Medicine, which is about integrating soul through personal development, embodiment, movement and dance, creativity and art. Cultivating a deeper connection to body, heart and mind and finding out from our own myth, we discover who we are.

We step into each of these gateways, gathering the tools and the resources that we need. Accepting and surrendering to where our soul must dwell at this time.

This Medicine Wheel not only supports our personal growth, but offers deeply healing experiences and meditations to open the heart and 're-member' a broken innocence, putting ourselves back together is how we 're-member' our completeness. We learn to use the tools that can physically put us in touch with our vocation, guidance that will support us on the journey and the very particular archetypal quality we might need to embrace.

Without careful observance and enquiry into knowing where we are in the cycle of our soul's offering, it is almost impossible to know what stage we are at and what we need to embody before we can fully move on to the next stage. We can do this with the support of our community, listening to each others' experiences and learning and growing together.

Often we can find ourselves trying to move on too quickly to the next stage before fully engaging and digesting the last stage. Thus meeting with the same challenges over and over again without fulfillment.

We learn, one step at a time. Patiently unfolding what is truly intended for us.

We take a journey around the Wheel in contemplation, through life experience and by sharing in workshops, webinars and gatherings. We can also use the Middle Earth Medicine Cards for divination, to inspire us along the way. To look at where we might need to gather more information, or to find what we are lacking in. The meanings and interpretations will be something different to each one of us. Nothing is set in stone.

For Those who lost their tongues

The Middle Earth – this holding land,
the indigenous of our tribe,
the people of my heritage,
their medicine
and their myths, where dragons and elves
not only in dreams.

As Kings fought for their forests,
the land,
the sacred medicine
where beasts and other-worlds live
as one
but those who burnt
at the stake,
and those who
lost their tongues
were silenced,
bloody and burnt.

I sat there,
She, at my back
stirring my own cauldron,
knowing when the time was right,
they would come
to listen, to know, to receive
the wisdom of the old one,
the witch, the crone

And she – the Seer,
through my eyes,

through my songs,
would touch those hearts
and that same medicine
that flows,
now at this time
the time that is right
for the empowerment of her voice
and the worlds of Middle-Earth
brought back to life
back to the hearts
of our own lineage

For I feel the wounds of my great, great, great grandmothers
and I dig my hands and my roots into their soil,
I sing the songs of those ancestors,
their voice will be freed through mine
and their screams 'will' be heard
and their wisdom will be – released

And those who have been forgotten
that flesh – and that bone
in my dreams will – be – remembered
for our ancestors need be sung
if we are meant to heal

And that soul of our humanity,
as the old one prays,
will return for sure
in that voice of mystery
mending the betrayal
of our broken ways.

The Heart of the Artist

Jungian psychology speaks of the need for us to honour our own human and innate archetypes, to allow them to express themselves through us. And if we do not live that quality into being, then we die – spiritually. These archetypes live within our unconscious self, often unfulfilled and under resourced.

This can lead to deep depression and hunger for acknowledgement. We might also be carrying trauma from the past, which leads us to shut down and adds to this depression. It can also cause hyper-vigilence, flight or fight tendencies as we become so guarded against the hurt that life can bring.

We fit ourselves into the world that feels safe, never reaching higher than the ground, never daring to meet the tree-tops and the skies, but staying close to the pavements and the shadows of our existence.

Shutting down our psyche and becoming numb are often associated with depression, with the underlying anxiety that this can bring.

What does it feel like when these parts of us are deadened to the world that we long to live in? De-pressed, forced inwards, shut down, unfeeling, un-creative, frozen in time.

There are no feelings as such, there is simply nothing there; a deadening of the soul, a hunger that cannot be filled. There is no sense of emotion, nothing that the heart can speak of, or sing of, or dance with. The body and heart, defeated, close down, barely able to eat or else stuffing food in until the stomach is fit to burst, or drinking alcohol in great quantities in a desperate attempt to disallow any pain that might want to start to seep through the opening cracks of despair.

We know in ourselves that a walk, a dance, a conversation with another will help us to overcome some of these sensations, but we are also unable to motivate ourselves to do this. No matter how many people tell us we 'should' be doing this, we simply cannot. So we stop talking to others, we stop communicating about the heart ache and we isolate ourselves so that no one can reach us, so the trauma continues to hold us in its grip. For this often does come with trauma, or neglect, or abuse in its many forms. Knowing how to reach into that place is not so easy. But it can also be because we are not living our passion, our soul purpose, our reason for being alive.

That archetype is dead inside us.

We need to find a sense of aliveness and vitality moving through the body so that we can actually feel the emotions that are needing to be released, to allow the visions to be noticed and brought into the realm of the living.

And how many of us put on that mask of being fine, of being okay, of being able to lie and pretend that there is no problem in our world?

Making it through life as if nothing has happened. Pushing through the dark place and yet deep within there is a numbness hiding away a hurting that is covered up so well, there is only a disappearing.

And thus a disappearing of the soul and the archetypal energy that is our birthright that longs to live and longs to love.

That steely stare will banish all that is possible and only death can reach that door.

It takes one to know this place and this crippling heartache to be able to reach in, to the cries from within the other.

So we start with a finger, a tiny movement, we pick up a pencil and we write the words 'I am here' and we write it over and over again, reminding ourselves that we really are alive. And then the words, or the pictures, begin to find their way onto the page. And whatever is in our heart begins to find its way into the world of the living. That piece of music, that artist's tale, that surrender to humanity, and hope and recognition becomes the fruit of this calling, to stretch our soul once more into its rightful place.

The archetype is living and remembering itself, whoever we are. No longer lost and caught in an unfeeling web, we learn to express and to reach out again. And if we can trust there is something so much greater than ourselves, that there is something so much greater than our own thinking mind and ego, then we can also reach out to that one, that God of our own understanding and we know we are loved and cared for again. Without this, with too much loneliness, where connection is hard to find, we too easily become lost once more.

And so with the support of knowing our archetype and its particular journey, we embrace the calling of our soul and in those moments of loss, we understand how much we are needed by others who live in such similar places and we begin to serve and support them into their own artistry.

When we tap into our own authentic archetype, our eco-identity, a new sense of presence is discovered and a new sense of purpose is revealed. And then we reveal how our rightful archetype, can support us into the Sovereign we were initially born as.

Our Middle Earth Medicine Wheel that I share here with you, takes us on a journey through those depths of heart, loneliness, even the deepest loss, reaching in to find that joy and vitality, to allow the emotions their freedom, their voice and their fullest, most creative expression. To bring alive the explorer, the hunter gatherer, and to live once again or even for the first time – fulfilled.

How do I dance myself into the world?
And embrace the courage to remove the mask
that no longer serves me?
The ancestral story that says
'I do not belong -
That I am too fragile for the world,
that my voice cannot be heard'
My sensitive being will not accept the call,
for it is too vulnerable to meet the world
Yet, for all it knows as the wisdom prevails
– it reminds itself

of the sacred contract
and it takes that one step that says
'yes'

Notes

Embodiment

Embodiment is a relatively new word that is used quite a lot these days, in dance, in yoga, in many movement and therapeutic processes. And yet it can mean something different to many people and can sometimes be quite misleading. It is often the way with words that we adopt. So I began to look up in dictionaries and the like, to see what we as the human race actually believe it to mean. I didn't see anything that said 'dance, heart, body'. Yet when I read about embodiment in a lot of presentations or marketing, I wonder what this word refers to, what is it trying to tell us? What exactly are we being asked to embody? This is one of the first questions we must ask.

So how does this affect what I am here to do, *and what exactly am I asking others to embody?* When I ask that question, I am immediately struck by how it affects me and what my response to it is. I am asking if people can really and truly embody themselves, fully and utterly. But what does it mean to really and truly embody yourself?

For me, it is to be able to embody your soul and your true identity. And we stumble across the same difficulty with that word soul, which although older than embodiment, is banded about a lot now without any true depth or understanding. I specialise in soul retrieval, it is my passion and my fascination, because I yearn to know with each individual what their own unique soul is. And as someone who has experienced soul loss, like the majority of us, I also know what it feels like to reclaim it and the absolute buzz of that!

What is the soul?

I believe it is the unique and innate part of us, that is not like, nor could be like, any other. It is our uniqueness that brings about our particular purpose. Our personality and archetype is formed by our existence and upbringing, but the soul comes way before that. And it is the return to that which is what the life journey, the myth of our life is about, except for many of us we have forgotten that vital part of living and made it more about surviving.

So my hope is that this book will explain much of what I mean about reclaiming the soul and living an embodied life. A life that supports the reclaiming of soul and becoming the person we really are here to be. That is what embodiment means to me, the inclusion of our fullness and knowing our mythological story as we embody it, digest it and bring it to life. All of our aspirations and creative juice included. Not a mundane life where there is no spark or no imagination. A sense of fulfilling one's innate purpose, to know oneself, to bring all of that knowing into manifestation – with the willingness to shine!

The Seer & Origins

And so I will share some of my story and how I found the Wheel and my own journey with soul embodiment.

* * *

Born on the winter solstice between the dark and the light, a middle child, with an older brother and a younger sister – I am in the middle, holding my own. Am I male? Sometimes, yes. I wear my brother's hand-me-downs, old jeans and trainers. I let him teach me football and rugby, as at times he has no other boys to play with, so I must. I fail at this sport – this sport that I can make no sense of. We ride our bikes together and find other means to live in connection, having fun as brother and sister should, according to our mother. He digs up old bones with me though and that suffices. They are the bones of our pets that had to be buried when they died. We look beneath the grave and find the oddments of bone and to this day they are resurfaced to make medicine tools and creative pieces of wonderment.

Living up to my big brother was part of my story that would help me to identify my role in this world.

Am I female? Sometimes, yes. The little girl who came after me needs her bigger sister to play those games that only girls will play. We find the dolls, cuddly toys, the dresses and a pram that goes rusty when we leave it in the garden on rainy days. There live slugs and snails taking refuge, seeking out the crumbs from our picnics. We put our rabbits and our guinea pigs in the pram and push them around the garden, singing little songs and donning them with white lacy baby hats tied under their chins.

I was introduced to jealousy in those days. I felt the curse begin to surface from under my skin and within my bones. She, that pretty thing, with the long golden hair and mine a strange reddish sort of ginger that Mother called titian blonde.

I cut it off once. My sister's hair, that is. One day, whilst left in the car at a parent-teacher meeting outside the school, I found a pair of scissors and that was that. I spent a long while in my bedroom 'contemplating' I am told.

So was I a boy or a girl? I could do both quite well it seemed. It was a useful way to merge in the world. One day dancing in my ballet classes and being amongst ponies and horses, and another with the boys on motorbikes, wearing leather jackets. My masculine and feminine sides developed quite well as I worked out how to hang out with the lads, the motor bikes and trips to biking events, as well as how to be 'correct' in my mother's world and wear nice dresses and be good at the all-girls' public school I went to. That was until they told me to leave.

I was not so well behaved. I seemed to find even the simplest tasks unnecessary. I found the work hard and as it was an expensive school, it was suggested kindly, that my parents were wasting their money!

Our home environment was a nice, middle-class family. Living in an abundant home with a garden in the Midlands. It was somewhere near the Black Country, where my father worked in factories as a director, an important role, running the family business. The Midlands seemed a good place to be. It held many adventures, from inner city life to the rural countryside that we eventually escaped to. It seemed to hold a good array of interest for me. I liked going between city and nature, nature and city.

I liked the factories with the machinery, the loud rhythmic sounds and the smell of sacking and oil. The voices of the working classes, who swore a lot, even in jest. I liked that. My mother would never allow such words. I even said a few myself, when I knew that she could not hear.

I put three-penny bits in the drinks machine and took them all cups of tea and coffee. I loved the smell of that dark, rich roast sitting in the red, plastic cut-out tray, splashed with coffee stains, it was a dirty brown, sticky in texture. And like the tray, that dark, rich roast seemed to have stained the workers' teeth too. Or perhaps it was the endless cigarettes they smoked indoors around the factory, marking little burns on the wooden frames around the machinery.

There was not so much noise from the traffic back then. Concrete walkways and graffiti everywhere, caught my attention.

Then there was the countryside, ah, sweet nature. The animals and the places to hide, the deep dark tunnels of the stately home on which we lived in the grounds of. All derelict, wrecked and ruined but a wonderful adventure playground for us as children.

The trees and the old hedgerows, the metal gates and a wonderment of elemental experiences, I could be here on my own with my animals. They understood me more than most, I felt.

I rode my pony, drove the old Land Rover and would ride my bike over rough land and through large puddles attempting not to get soaked. We climbed trees and in and through hay barns, visited horses in neighbouring fields, taking them apples from orchards when no one was watching. We borrowed a little rowing boat from the shores of the lake and paddled out into the centre, daring each other to jump in and swim. It was a deep, dark lake, many a mother's concern.

The gypsies lived over the hill and they were my closest friends in those parts. I rarely chose friends that met with a parent's approval, always looking for those a little out on the edge of society. It seemed to be my way. I knew I was different, certainly very different to my family. This difference felt needed somehow. It would serve me well in life; understanding that part that felt separate, or less than, or just simply different, gaining from it the resources that would keep me focused on a spiritual healing path. We often hear that it takes one person in the family to be the 'black sheep' to be the one that wakes up the 'comfortable normality' of family life, to awaken what lies in the shadows and draw out a little more of the truth. Whatever the truth in this, I was certainly that one. Difficult though it may have been for myself and the others, it certainly showed me a thing or two about family life and what my part was in it. At this time in my life, the time of adolescence, my mythological story was beginning to unfold.

I would come to learn more about this over time, what it was that made me different and what I would in time discover was a deeper connection to the edge walking that was a part of my life, that included my connection to spirituality.

I am ever grateful for my understanding of God, for the faith I have carried, the particular spiritual path that I find myself on and for its teachings and spiritual awakenings.

Sent to a Catholic school, though knowing myself as a Church of England, Protestant-reared child – I became confused as to why I wasn't fully accepted in this place. Forced to sit outside the sweet chapel with its plush purple carpets and rosary beads that the other students all seemed to handle in a certain way. The hard stone slabs outside, the feeling of coldness when I sat upon them, it felt unfair and humiliating. Having to go to the 'special' Protestant religious education classes while the good Catholic girls went to their 'special' classes. Why was I so in-between these beliefs? At home we went to church on a regular basis. It felt different to school assembly and only led to more confusion.

This was another place of opposites, caught between two churches, the polarity of religions. Yet my own beliefs and spirituality would find their way, to become what was right for my own existence.

With my children – three boys and three girls – I stand again in the middle of the masculine and feminine. It is a polarity of my own making – a balance of motherhood, holding this youthful energy field. I created and brought human beings into this world, each one with his or her many gifts and soul offerings. I watched them grow into theirs, knowing they were teaching me about mine. So fully, so deeply, so determinedly, so 'matter-of-factly'. Ordinary lives meeting ordinary lives.

Middle Earth continued through the dance as I balanced one life with another and I became the dance of my own opposites and polarities. These polarities tore me apart, as my yang energy urged me out into the world of dance, theatre and teacher trainings. And my yin mother instinct pulled me back into the nest to nurture my young.

As a favourite teacher once told me, 'There are two kinds of spirituality – one is parenting, the other is everything else!'.

It was a balancing act for sure. Cast in the middle of that vibration, I found my way to hold its life force and become the one who stood in the centre of that Mandorla, no matter how it made me feel. I felt the tearing apart of two worlds and what was being asked of me.

Yet this tearing apart was to create within me the deepest and most soulful experience I could ever have known, yet did not know at that time. This was me meeting my edge and walking that edge through life. It would be my mission and I would learn to hold it well in this particular world, mastering its effect by not falling too fully into one world or the other.

Separate and yet in the middle of all of these opposites in my life.

Imagine holding two polarities in each hand and finding a balance between them. What does that feel like, deep inside?

This was the growing up of my life. And over time, I began to see each with more clarity, a deeper understanding and was able to stand up and say, 'I know and understand how polarity affects us!'.

I visited births and deaths and I learnt about this most timely spectrum of life. The beginnings and the ends, and oh, how I love beginnings and endings.

Many deaths came my way and many births... Learning what death is and what birth is; I learnt so much about their meeting place.

And then I looked through all the different stages of my life. I saw the archetypal qualities and energies that had served me in the births and the deaths and the pathway that had opened up to the creativity of my life.

I documented it carefully.

And when holding a vision quest for others one day, I saw its map, its tree of life and its own particular model of work. This is what became, 'The Wheel Of Soul's Return'.

This was my story, from my journey with the Wheel, when I examined what was really mine to do. Here lay the potential of my own vocation and soul's calling. What unfolded then was how I could offer it back to others.

Innocence to Sovereignty

And so we begin to learn about our own journey. The return of the soul and the path from innocence to sovereignty. A simple map to help us bring our innocence, our Golden Crown, back to the realm where it was first bestowed.

I share some of my discoveries along with my own story, as this is how I came to create the Wheel and find its offering and how useful it could be.

Take note as we journey together, play with the cards, explore what is yours and be the Seer of your own life story. What is the myth that you hold?

Notes

And So, Beyond the Veil

Before we are born we are but a dream; a star amongst many others. A vision is created in that universal atmosphere of love and the sacred contract begins to define itself.

What will we be? Who will we be? And what will be expected from us?

With that comes the dream of our own soul. It is the sacred contract that dreams itself into being as we make our journey closer to Earth.

The Dreamer will begin to call forward much of this story, reclaiming the knowledge that is needed to truly live our life.

I have witnessed that every time I have created something, whether it be a project or a piece of work; it began as a dream.

My own dreamer would begin receiving images and ideas, not always knowing where they came from. Then, my innocent, curious nature would take the dream into my hands, playing with this new image or idea, allowing that curiosity to manifest in a form that filled me with fascination.

Might I ignore my own dreams?

Might I dare to open to the possibility that I can dream big, that I can say a simple 'yes' to the dream that is so rooted within my own myth?

This I had to take care of and at times I know I need to ask others what they see, for I am not the all-knowing. I cannot allow my own arrogance to always assume I am right, even when it is my own life. The effect I have on others around me must be looked after.

* * *

I was born in Birmingham in 1960 to a mum who yearned for a little girl and she was so happy when I was born. Here was the perfect little girl that she dreamt of having.

She already had a son – a sweet-natured little boy. So the perfect family had arrived.

My mother seemed like a perfectionist to me. I had a sense that she liked everyone else to see us as perfect, especially the neighbours, other members of our family, and anyone who she attended particular ladies' groups with, like Tupperware parties and that sort of thing.

It seemed, however, that my mother would need to hide quite a bit from the world. I did not play that perfect daughter from the early age of six months. Sadly, that was not to be. This created conflict in the family; how, for my mother, to present the 'perfect' when all was anything but.

I could go into a lot of details, about the demanding nature I adopted, the screams and tantrums, and the need she had to lock me in my bedroom on countless occasions. But it feels unnecessary to go into all of that. I have no regrets, because this information has, in many ways, helped me to build a better picture of my own life. But please note, I do not in any way condone any form of brutal, abusive behaviour towards children, nor would I lock a child in her bedroom when acting out. I believe this need in a child is a cry for some sort of attention. The child is troubled and does not understand what is going on.

I was indeed in need of something. There was a shadow in my family and my parents were not the most well-equipped to deal with it. That was back in the '60s, things were somewhat different. So I also want to stress that I do not have any bad feelings towards my mother for the way she handled me, the struggles she had with me and how things came to pass. For without my own unique story, I would not be writing this book now.

I love both my parents dearly and since their passing I have missed them immensely.

There is an issue to raise that there would literally be no point in living a life of regret, of resentment or as a victim of my upbringing. That would be a life wasted. So I need to face my own story and look into the gold and treasure that lies there.

Turning the darker aspects and shadow of my innocence into something useful has been a creative process.

I also need to look at my own part in the continuance of negative patterns, where I made ongoing mistakes myself. I also need to see where I have created a belief or a story out of something in the past, when it wasn't really that way at all!

Our memories fade. We tell a story over and over. And in time it can become something that it is not, yet the feelings around it grow stronger. I have had to train myself (or even be trained) to look at the truth of the situation and to only work with the facts. What really happened, what was really going on, do I remember it exactly as it was? Only then can I piece the story together, acknowledge the truth, allow the emotion and move on.

The most interesting thing for me is that there was quite a bit of comparison between my brother and I. I was compared to him by my mother and I then began to compare my own abilities with his. Was I as clever, as able, as strong, as intelligent? I surrendered to this, giving up on occasions when I just simply could not compete. It was not his fault in any way, just circumstance within our family. But it was a strong part of my story, one that troubled me at first, but one that I was also able to turn around into something positive for myself.

My mother told me a tale some years ago about when my brother first went to school; this, for me, is a very interesting part of the story!

On my brother's return from his first day at school, he came home and wrote his name on a piece of paper for our mother. Her reaction, as she explained it to me, was not just to be happy for him, but to feel she had not been a good enough mother by not teaching him to write his name (and probably much more) before he actually attended his first school. What a great mum the teacher would have thought she was! And what an incredibly intelligent child she would have!

But it hadn't been this way and that had saddened her.

So, at the tender age of three, my mother got to work to teach me the alphabet. She ensured that I learnt words, began to read and write and most definitely that I was able to write my own name.

So I would attend my first day at school, with reading and writing well under my belt! The teacher of course would be very impressed. I would be even more the perfect young lady my mother dreamt of.

I didn't know at the time but this was a very necessary part of my own calling, to be a writer. But not any kind of writer – a poetic kind of a writer. And how this would come about, well, it would take a long time to unfold.

But it did, because by the time I was five years old, I had a passion for poetry, writing prose and verse, and music and dancing. It seemed to be a sort of accumulation of creativity that went together.

I believe it was possibly the only way I could write from a voice of innocence. A muddling together of words and phrases, of broken grammar, missed punctuation, fantasy, and sentences that came from somewhere other than a mind well-versed. Rather it came from a spirit connection, a making up, a letting things flow, a remembering something of my own dreaming. A curious imaginative mind where words and made-up-meanings filtered through a channel of emptiness and not really knowing.

Still it flowed and I loved the feeling that went with it. It excited me and I persevered.

To this day I get that same feeling, as my fingers write or type across the page. I let go just as in the dance. I let things flow, no censoring, and no trying to figure it all out.

No, do not read over those words. Do not be influenced by what is already written. Simply keep moving forward, until that second wind is reached just as in any marathon. When the energy courses through the veins and the creative spirit, where the words become heaven sent, it is not possible to hold back.

The horse reaches for those stars and the poetry has no stumble to fall onto, a clear sky where all is revealed and the poem is created.

The editing and 'putting right' can come later. This is verse from spirit. This is a no-mind state when my heart opens a little wider. My flesh tingles, I feel my own heart beat and I am transported into another world. My focus is intent and there is nothing to do but dance my fingers across the page. This is creative writing, giving permission to the spirit of this energy.

I cannot really do it any other way, nor ever could.

Back to school, I'm sure the teachers were mildly impressed, but they took it upon themselves to get me to do it the way it 'should' be done, in the Queen's English, grammar exact and proper punctuation.

I had other plans.

My mother's need for perfection was gradually dismissed and I rebelled. The tantrums, if I can call them that, or high energy, some upsetting force not recognised, got worse. And I was labelled, simply, a rather difficult child, whose school report said, 'Could do better!'.

Was there a reason for all of this? My way of writing was being developed at that very early age, with an innocent view of the world and a connection through dance and poetry. A make-believe kind of existence that only I could feel if I found God and I prayed and danced. This was part of our upbringing too. We had to pray.

And as I found with that creativity, is it possible that something was being dreamt through me? Had I remembered just a little of my own purpose in life, my own mythological character? When I listen to what truly makes me happy this lifetime, it's writing, publishing a book – especially a poetry book, but also being the truth teller and the wordsmith.

And I know and feel absolutely sure – if we are to know our vocation – it is what makes us happy. It is what we know in our heart is ours to do, what fills us with joy.

The dream is alive in us and it needs our elders to recognise that in its truest form. I cannot know if my mother sensed any of this, but when she bought me the biggest poetry book possible one Christmas called 'The Golden Treasury Of Poetry', perhaps there was a glint of knowing and she needed to encourage this.

Still, I also sat in the psychiatrist's chair as my mother, convinced there was something wrong with me (and right she may have been, though wasn't looking in quite the right direction), had me analysed and studied, to quieten her own mind.

So this seems to be the start of my own dreaming, but I would not awaken to it until much later in life. And when the awakening started to happen, I reclaimed this story, as part of my journey into sovereignty, into my mytho-identity.

Dreaming Ourselves Awake

This work takes us from the beginning of an awakening dream. Those moments that wake us up, that we feel the tremors of, letting us know that a new journey is beginning. If we look into our life story, there is a chance that we will see how the awakening is likely to play itself out. What will be new, what will we discover? And what will support us as we go on this journey? It will also show us the patterns that may not serve us, the repetitions that may need to change and the habits that cause dysfunction in our world.

If we can imagine that our life story and the life of our vocation, project or art, run as parallel time-lines together, then we see that the journey of our life will inform the journey of our soul, as we inhabit our purpose or awaken our vocation. Thus The Wheel Of Soul's Return is designed to be a visual archetypal representation of these parallels, representing both the life story and the purposes story.

What can we learn about how to inhabit the soul, from the story of how we came to live and be on the earth and what it has all entailed?

So how do we Dream Ourselves Awake?

Our original purpose that we brought to earth is often lost beyond a veil of illusion. A smoke filled mind and fog will hide the view of what we once knew. But this is a necessary forgetting, because it is the sculpting of our life that will carve out the necessary and perfect requirements for us to fulfil that purpose.

We will need to do our own healing before we embark on trying to heal others. We will need to resource ourselves with the right information before we try to resource others with any of our ideas or understandings. We will need to change our own circumstances before we try to change others. We will need to walk ahead on the path, so that we can lead another to their sanity or sobriety.

Some will come to this place, but some will remain without any change or movement forward, unable to find their way through the quagmire of circumstances. Some will die never having fulfilled that purpose or even trying to. We may never consider the changes that need to happen, always fixated on 'one' way fits all.

We need courage to change the things that we can.

It is the knowledge of our purpose that can be dormant and asleep. So in order to awaken it, we must simply ask, 'What is mine to do?' And then watch, follow, open ourselves to the possibilities of change, step into unknown territories and take a few risks we may never have taken before.

We will start to awaken, sometimes quickly, sometimes slowly, but if our intention is good, if we are coming from a good place inside, then we cannot help but step onto that pathway that there is no going back from!

Once we ask those questions and we step onto that path, those moments, memories and experiences that are beautifully and divinely sculpted can come in many forms, some challenging and some in moments of celebration. They can happen for many reasons. Usually they come later in life, when we are resourced enough to manage them and are able to seek guidance and support, but not necessarily always.

I experienced awakenings during the dance, during my writings and during other times of creativity. They have happened within meditations, during a walk in the park, or in conversation with another person, maybe a therapist or counselor.

What has been made clear to me from my own experience is that it is always the perfect time, even if it feels as if it isn't.

I have never had an awakening that I could not handle, even if it was painful. I had to trust that they just wouldn't happen if I wasn't strong enough or didn't have the resources to cope. After all, my life journey tells me I have experienced this once before and if I have digested and learnt from that story, then I am able to learn from that experience and I am here to tell that tale.

What is a spiritual awakening?

A spiritual awakening is a moment in time when we get to see something about ourselves or our life that has an impact on our psyche. We have a revelation, an in-sight, and a realisation. This might be experienced as immense joy but often as shock, awkwardness or even embarrassment. It might be part of a story that we have perceived as negative, that has troubled us. We may have taken a victim's point of view. Yet we begin to see value in it as it teaches us greater skills at managing our life or reclaiming part of the brokenness.

Whatever way it is received, it is not usually all that comfortable. Light is illuminating a part of us that we have never seen before, part of our ego that would have preferred to remain hidden, unknown, not wanting to be seen!

Sometimes we remember the old, old story and its memory held in the body. It begins to emerge, emotion comes with it, the energy is released and we 'feel'.

What that feeling is will be different for everyone and for every circumstance. Sometimes it can be very painful to bear and tears may come to our eyes. Sound might come from deep in the belly. We may remember wrong-doings, we may remember awkward things that we are ashamed of, or we may remember something that was done to us that we are very uncomfortable with.

The realisation takes us into the belly or gut where the pain can be deep. Our heart opens and if we are willing and feel safe enough, we can express what that means to us. If we feel unsafe, judged or likely to receive ridicule, then we may shut it away and refuse to acknowledge it. It might then disappear from view, once more underneath the bedspread of our inner world. It remains unconscious.

We might try to justify it, to rationalise it and this will take us away from possible growth and the spiritual awakening that is being made available to us.

It is ultimately our choice to do with this information as we wish. But if we refuse the awakening spirit and the potential of new growth, we will remain small and inferior to our fellow men and women.

If we choose to awaken, we will become lighter in step and in spirit, humble to the call and inspired to live our life fully.

We adopt the wisdom of the Seer – the one who can see into our lives – and become more aware and open to where we are really going and what it is that we are here to do and become. That one light and that one soul, ready to embrace the potency of our life on this earth.

The awakenings are always timely. They do not happen at a time when it would not be possible to receive it. Some may never recognise that call however, using substance to push it away and bury it down because the pain is too great, maybe the pain or fear of being seen, the fear of failure or simply for our light being too bright! But the deeper it is buried, the more painfully it will have to be re-called.

If this is taken to death, the soul never fully lives its life and can never inhabit the human body fully. There is a refusal to bear this light. To realise who one truly is, and the mind takes over. The ego becomes too big and the negative spirit of the chosen substance will rule!

And it is only the one who can humble themselves at some point, to let go of the need to be alone with their difficulties, to lean into something greater and more powerful than their own ego, who can ask for help. The one who can surrender to the source, to where they came from and learn to trust in the greater scheme of things. This is what it means to trust. To trust fully without a doubt that there is something greater watching over us and wanting us to fulfill our purpose.

There comes a time to be with others. To allow their reflections to be a mirror to one's own journey. To receive support and a hand to hold, to cry those tears of memory, to let go of the holding on, to let God in. To surrender to the pain that can and will live in us if we do not.

Our will-power will ruin us if we do not surrender at some point, trusting that there is another way to live.

Once that surrender and trust in the experience has occurred, that pain released and the burden dropped, it becomes easier to embrace the surrender and we get to know the resources we need to support our awakenings. We choose the right kind of people to nurture and support us. We dig deeper because we know that the energy received will propel us even further into a bountiful existence. More love, more acceptance, more kindness towards our vulnerability and our soul.

We choose our community and friends well, for they cannot in any way collude with our ego. This will not serve us. So we find those who understand the 'aha' moments when that light bulb is switched on. We choose them because they listen and do not judge, they do not try to fix us or make suggestions. They might share their own experience with us if we ask them, but that must be all there is if we are to grow and they are willing to support that growth. For we never know what the needs of others are, as we cannot know what is right for them. Therefore we listen, we observe, we check in with our own hearts and we act in service to the other in the best way possible.

We would hope to have many spiritual awakenings, as this softens us, allows our vulnerability and helps us to embody the essence of our true nature.

In recognising and sharing my own path, continually doing my best to reclaim my soul with all its potential, I find I am in a position to support others on their own awakening journey. I listen, I share my story and my own experience.

Without fulfilling my own purpose, I would be useless at this. Having an understanding of what this means is vital as I could not help others without being willing to also witness their pain and not try to fix it. To witness without trying to find the answers, for that would mean me playing God in their lives. They cannot grow with my intrusion. They can only grow if they are witnessed and honoured for 'their own intelligence' on this journey.

Our dream has awakened in us and it is time to get to know it in its fullness, it shook us, we remembered and now it becomes the time to look deeper at how it melds with the story of our life already lived.

* * *

I believe that everything begins with a dream, an awakening moment, a thought, a memory, like that flash in the dark or a light bulb moment. Our minds are clever, they pick up those thoughts and images and we either turn away from them or we listen and observe, sometimes acting irrationally on them, sometimes being a bit too unrealistic without checking what is right for our own and others' highest good. But dream we do, and awaken to our highest potential that we all have the opportunity to accomplish.

This, then, is drawn into life by our curious, innocent nature.

Innocence Reclaimed

When I danced as a child I didn't have a practice to do except when I went to a ballet school where I learnt steps and a variety of exercises. I was about three years old when I began those classes, and they went on until my teens. This gave me good poise and discipline at that time.

But when my teacher gave us free reign to dance our own dance, then my heart opened and I took great advantage of that moment, when my body danced to its own rhythm, to its own beat and every part of my body leapt into alive-ment.

I felt free and knew that I was meeting with something much greater than myself.

It was like a holy union, a power, a life force and I loved it. There were times where I felt I could dance out of my body, when I could escape from how I felt and be at one with God, where nothing else existed, just a place of peace and where I was free.

And then there were times when I would gather all that I needed from the dance, bringing it more fully to earth, allowing it to show me a little more about why I was here. I would write, whatever flowed from my heart, onto the page.

As I grew older, I learned that I could be distracted in the dance and be taken away from that holy union. And so I learned to discipline myself and stay focused and connected to that life force, to my body, my bones and the moving muscles. This was meditation, to stay with that singular intent throughout my dance.

And it was at these times that I felt the strength of my body, a muscular toning, and a vibration that I felt at no other time.

This I learnt was a quickening of the soul!

I can bring all the distraction with me, take heed of it. What is it that would disrupt this moment, what is it that I would make more important than my connection to spirit?

What was it that tried to pull me away from my dance?

Knowing and understanding this would give me more fuel to dance with and ignite me further into that vibration of light, making me more determined to meet what I truly needed. And that is and was my connection to God and to the truth. To fill my life with goodness, a healthy direction, the simple task of living in service and a mind that thinks clearly about the next right thing to do.

When I hear music or a beat there is a quickening inside me, it moves me, wherever I am. My heart will beat with it and I might remember that dance floor I was on previously, or feel my feet tapping for a moment. It fills me with joy and I know my connection more deeply, more closely with that holy union. When music touches my soul I know that I am here to dance and to create, just as I did as a small child and as a teenager and well into my fifties, nearly sixties, as I finalise this book in my sixtieth year.

I know I am here to support finding the creative medicines that our culture needs, to bring that quickening into others' lives and into the hearts and souls of those who have become absent and those who have lost touch with their innocence. I know I am here to support others in doing their inner work, in being there for those who are breaking. I know the places some have gone to, it is serving me to serve them. To share my experiences with them and to listen with compassion and without judgement. To help the soulless reclaim what is rightfully theirs and to find out who they truly are.

For those where soul-retrieval is the only way forward and no other remedy will do.

* * *

As I grew up in a very religious family, I knew I had a strong connection to God, to Spirit and all that it meant to me at that very young age. I prayed and I spoke with God about all of my troubles and walked country lanes asking questions, expecting them to be answered. I developed my own sense of spirituality that I knew was quite different to that of my parents and school teachers, including the nuns in the convent and this suited me just fine.

My relationship with God did often have to be on my terms however, which was not so healthy. Still, I was always comforted to know that I had this connection and I knew how to pray, and that it gave me the comfort I often needed.

I experienced my animals, my pets, as being part of that spiritual journey and felt that they had a soul. Yet the nuns in school told me that animals had no soul and did not go to heaven. I had to refuse this information.

My connection to animals, to the toys in my bedroom, the objects on my shelves, the music I played, even the food I ate – everything was 'real'. I believed that everything had a soul.

* * *

I am on a journey in Ireland. I have been on a mission to heal some old wounding, as well as sharing a workshop with a group of dancers. A part of me has opened up and is very connected to my innocence. There is a need; a sadness. Something to unravel and I know it is connected to my childhood.

I walk a small street in an Irish town, where in a shop window I notice a grey toy rabbit. I see it, fallen from the shelf and flopped over next to the wall and the window. At that moment I recognise myself, fallen and lost and the rabbit speaks to me, 'I am lost too, I need help!' I hear it so clearly! Going into the shop, I ask the shopkeeper for the rabbit in the window. He says there are many of the same rabbits on the shelf in the shop and I should pick one of them. I ask him, 'please can it be that rabbit in the window?'

I knew in my heart I could not abandon that one. He reluctantly fetches the rabbit, clambering around in the shop window until he can reach it and my rabbit friend is saved. I thank the shopkeeper.

Wrapped in purple tissue paper, I return with the rabbit to my son's house where I am staying. My granddaughter is there and in my bag I have a present for her, which I take out and she is delighted with.

My grey rabbit, wrapped in its purple-tissue, lies in that same bag, but I know I must not take it out. It is not the right time and if I do, my granddaughter for sure will need to take rabbit to her room to live amongst her other teddies. And this is not what I intended for my new friend.

So little rabbit lies in my bag.

After a few days I am to visit another friend, Sally, who is a bodyworker. I do not trust many with my body but with her I am able to put myself into her care. And as her hands go to work, I am pulled back to the memories of sadness and the wound I was feeling at that earlier time. There are deep sobs within me and I find the expression of what needs to move.

I recalled a memory; turning up day after day at the school gate, always with an object in my hand or under my arm. I believed its soul was speaking to me, and it needed attention. I needed it also, some small amount of comfort to help me through my day in this alien place. I did not want to be alone. Other children would tease me at the school, making jokes about me always having to have something with me.

I remember two girls standing at the school gate waiting to see, 'Has she got something precious?' They would jeer unkindly and then run away laughing when they saw that of course I had, no matter how hard I tried to disguise it.

This did lead to being a bit of a hoarder, a collector, which happily is far more in check these days. Still, my very first rabbit, a red and white one, given to me on the first day of my birth by my maternal grandmother, sits in pride of place in my bedroom. And he is not the only one of my childhood toys!

Everything had its own uniqueness and even to this day I can sense the 'realness' of all things, of everything having soul. This makes for a huge amount of grief within one's heart, to bear the pain of all that is misused and the pain and suffering of the soul of our humanity.

Where does that pain lead us?

And so, as I lay on the mattress receiving the healing from my friend, my heart opened and I heard a calling,

'Give yourself a present' it said, 'Nourish that innocent part of you and accept what you know and understand about life.'

I asked my friend to pass me my bag. And from it, I pulled out the little parcel of purple tissue paper, opening up the gift of the little grey rabbit. And holding it close to my heart, I cried. I spoke to my friend about how painful it could be, to not be understood and how I had not been able to abandon the little rabbit in the corner of the window, how I needed it to come with me.

It had represented part of me that just needed a caring hug, a moment in time that said, 'It's ok, I am here.' I began to learn how to take this sort of action as a way to look after myself and became aware of something I had seen from earlier years – a need to reclaim my innocent nature.

I learnt much more about this little fur ball as time went on and how I had held a need for it in my life. It was a route to me healing my own innocence and bringing that part of me back to life. For it was my own innocence that I was feeling; the broken hurt one, the one that needed to find a way back to the body and live life as God had intended me to live it.

* * *

I have always been fascinated with what spirituality and shamanism shows us. And at the core root, it shows me the animistic nature of all things.

I have recognised this same feeling in so many aspects of my life, seeing and sensing spirit and soul in all things, recognising my connection and need for something outside myself. Being almost possessed by callings and needing to take care of inanimate objects because they have deeper meanings, because they are part of a ritual yet to be danced or spoken.

My drum, my second skin, my beating heart, is just as an animal, needing comfort, warmth, deep love and caring from me. I cannot ignore these sensations that in their turn awaken my own senses to something much bigger than me.

Spirituality existed for so many, in years gone by, within nature and within what could be seen and felt. It is part of our ancient heritage where there are so many theories on animism and shamanism. What is true and what is right?

The only thing I can be clear about is my own life and my own experience. I will all too easily isolate myself, become deeply melancholic, live on the edge of existence and become fascinated with my own mysteries, my beliefs in the spiritual realms and universal laws.

And with this I can avoid at all costs being 'one with the herd!' This does not make me right, it might mean I am seen as an oddball and I remind myself of this obscure nature, knowing I am not the only one! I have plenty to do to take stock, to reassess, to work on different parts of myself, to enable me to mix with ordinary society. I am not so 'different', I can just all too easily make myself that way and that isolates me more.

My job is to be a part of, not separate to, my kin. To do my work and to take what I can into the world of the other, without forcing my beliefs on them, without trying to fix and sort out. To humble myself to the world and blend in, with one gentle thought after another.

Patterns emerge and my own
sobriety forces me inward
To touch a soul less troubled
To know the change that I can
no more enforce than I can
understand the true meaning
behind that affliction

How it troubles me is not anyone
else's concern but my own
And that is what leads me on this journey
To heal my wound that
spurs me to change another
For my comfort I seek
For my solace I seek
And once beneath that desire
I can see with an open heart
The true need
The love and compassion
Without trying to fix – the one
Returning to myself I am drawn
to make that change
and lessen the load that speaks of enabling
so much to learn
so much to take in
and such a deep place to love

Notes

Wounded Innocence

What happens to a child that has been abused, neglected or traumatised, who later in life is trying to deal with that story? Remembering the 'whatever happened' and not just what happened in those moments but also what happened around the abuse, the words spoken and unspoken, the relationships to others, the stories hidden? Whether it is sexual abuse, verbal abuse, emotional abuse, they all have their stories.

Chances are that in those moments the child learned to dissociate, to lose presence and disappear. The child became ungrounded, which might have appeared as extreme shyness, overt confidence (even bully like) or self centredness. It may have presented as an inability to speak out, a need to steal, to hide, to shut oneself away, to constantly try to please others, the need to self-harm.

The child or young adult loses confidence and there is a problem with self esteem as they grow.

Shame and guilt ensue
and the spiral into
those deep pits of darkness
where the pain is felt
with no way out,
no way to claw
ourselves back
to the rim of light,
we sink deeper

where no hunger
will ever bring us out.
Lost to a story
that no one can hear,
because we dare not tell it,
for fear,
for fear of what?

In order to reclaim connection to the body and overcome the dissociation, body contact is needed. This is a physical necessity for any human; touch, verbal communication, body connection, a simple hug. But who can the child trust? Certainly not the adult world, for it is usually the adult world that has been the perpetrator of the abuse, or has not protected the child in the first place.

What does the child reach out to?

Something other than adults, or humans even. Possibly, the child looks to what is innocent that he can trust. What he sees as that part of himself that is lost.

This might be other children or it might be an animal, and often is. The need to cuddle a kitten, or a soft toy.

The child can begin to feel again, to be close to something, finding that it supports that reconnection to life, to warmth, to body comfort. This can help for a while, but is the ultimate need fulfilled? There will be a longing for more.

And then what if the child is teased for always needing something to be attached to. If she is denied those objects?

So she lets it go, hides the need away, makes it into something else that is not so obvious. Food, alcohol, sex, drugs, smoking? And sometimes she is drawn to possessions. She becomes materialistic, hunting for the next fix, something to buy, to own, to fill a hole she cannot fill any other way.

Over time the inner-child accumulates things. Purchasing those items that are tangible, material. The objects are not really needed, yet one feels a sense of belonging or of owning something. Something that can be trusted, not taken away, not ridiculed, something that is not harmful.

She then feels alive again, the emptiness diminishes for a while, she feels reconnected. She can feel her skin and her body and she can feel safe for that moment.

When shock arises, because it will re-emerge if the story is not remembered, understood and fully digested, then a hug from another may not feel ok. As it may have demands and conditions. 'What will I need to give back?' the child might ask. Does this come without those conditions?

The child's mind is unsure and fear follows along with the need to understand, the need to heal. And so the cycle continues, reaching out for inanimate objects or something that makes the child feel alive again.

The dissociation might still linger, but she can bring herself back through touch, the touch of her child's hand, or her grandchild's cuddles. But she cannot 'use' this for her own healing, it would not be right for the innocent one to be used in this way. So she reaches out for a new cushion, a new dress, an item for the kitchen, something that feeds the need to have and to hold.

What she must learn is a new way to trust, to not depend on something that she can do further harm with, or by endless purchasing. She can fill her home and gather possessions, as our earth is further used as a resource for what we do not really need. And the cycle turns, as more and more plastic and waste is thrown into our oceans from the need to heal the child within.

We are all shocked and wounded in some way, and we all have different ways of trying to stay embodied and to feel whole and alive.

How do we find our way to do what is necessary and our own unique way to be in life? That depends on our own particular personality, it also depends on the wounding of our own innocence.

This work is all about the reclaiming of that innocence, not to be that child again, but to embody the purity of spirit and to release the burden of carrying around with us the pain, humiliation and distrust that the wound inflicted on us in the first place.

And so as we step further towards our sovereignty, we begin to stop telling the story of victimhood, the 'poor me' stories. And we learn to find out who we were born to be without the unnecessary baggage. It is a long journey that cannot be overcome overnight. It takes careful unwrapping and gentle coming to terms with the horror that may have been such a large part of our growing up. Trying to understand it might make us fall back, for some it is impossible to understand why we would have been treated in a certain way. But we are here to overcome, to heal and to make a difference in our lives. To know that the stories we hold of our healing will inevitably be of value to others, once we have digested them ourselves and come to a healthier place with them.

Whatever we have experienced, we can be sure, has a deep connection to our own and others' healing path.

We cannot support others with our stories until we know our own life journey and can be accepting of that journey. We cannot go on the path with another, holding their hand or wanting their growth, if we are not able to share something with them that helps to bring their soul back or to help reclaim what is missing. My companion may need to hear from me how I have tackled a particular problem, or how I have steadied myself in one of those life storms! I may be able to share how taking a more grounded approach to something served me better than before. Sometimes it is as simple as sharing what it was that helped us.

The challenge to overcome and grow into sovereignty despite our wounds makes us stronger and more resilient in the end. It means we then have a tool bag of offerings for others in similar circumstances.

Our journey around the Middle Earth Medicine Wheel supports us to find this healing, to enable reconnection to what came before the abuse, the neglect or the dysfunction.

It supports us to release ourselves from creating more harm, to ourselves and others, to drop dysfunctional behaviour and the overprotective and hyper-vigilant parts of ourselves. To know it was not our fault that we were brought up in some of the ways that we were and that we played no part in it as children. To then grow from our life story, to start to reclaim our creative and beautiful self. To honour it, to allow its dream to unfold and begin to create from it, until it supports us to stand fully in service for the good of all.

Then we become sovereign. Then we find our wisdom and the joy that means we are alive, and we can enter the adult world free of our guilt and shame.

A Soul Free of Shame

Shame came to me as a beautiful woman,
No longer banished to an ugly tower,

She came to me as a beautiful woman
Free of the shackles and chains that would
bind her,

Shame came to me as a beautiful woman
Full of her own creative wisdom,
Free to dance and sing with her own voice.

Shame came to me as a beautiful woman,
No longer cast out as a memory of dysfunction

My spirit of shame, becomes that beautiful woman.

And this is where we find the dance so supportive towards our growth. We begin to reconnect to the body, to our own body. We become creative with it and we learn to allow our emotions to move more freely through it.

Only we can dance this dance, for it is our dance to dance and our healing to make matter. We become more embodied, more centred and if we so wish, we begin to find that connection once more to God, to Spirit. It is where the soul can reach us once again because we become free of the shackles, the limitations and the beliefs that we are not whole. But of course, this is not always an easy ride, not like it might be for some, for those who had less abuse in their history.

In the pain of my own body I feel your eyes
Encouraging me to open more and share those dark secrets from within
Searching for the unlimited stories that have lurked in the corners
Time forgotten on all sides
Ready to emerge to envelop me with shadows of dances not yet danced
And my feet move down into the ground
Spreading my roots into the earth
Saying hold me connect me support me
Here I go once more releasing the unnecessary burdens seeking fire to burn and rid me of the past and its melancholy
Surrendering to the fluidity of mighty rivers to wash away the pressure of having to live my life
To give it up is a timely and appropriate feeling

To live no more in dread of what may or may not come

My hurt, not yours, watch me yes

But do not rob me of my own power to heal myself

It is mine and given freely for me to use as I desire

Do not make yourself the rescuer, do not make yourself the healer

For that is your healing to let go of

This dance is my doing and mine alone

Simply see me and hold me in your gaze, see the darkness of me as well as my beauty

For here it unfolds on to the picture called 'my life'

The painting rich of many colours and textures

I am maiden, mother, warrior and crone, the wise woman in each

I am all these things and will be all for you

Whenever you need the dance, the eyes of connection

The witness of our truth, I see you

Yes I do see you, you young innocent one who had to leave trauma behind as best you could. And I know the part of you that has been stunted in your growth towards life and living. I know the part of you who feels broken inside, that finds it so hard at times, to let your inner light shine.

That creative life force stamped out of you, even though others say that you are talented beyond measure. You see, they simply do not know!

I know what you go through every single day. That crevice, hidden in the darkest cave, you dare not let it out. Where did that abuse come from? Sometimes we do not even know. Because at times it was so normalised and made so ordinary

Notes

This Middle Earth's Innocence

The new Middle Earth still exists in this modern world, where mystery and dreaming are being brought back into the arena of our daily living. The old Middle Earth became neglected and misunderstood in the past, and disbelieved. It became inconvenient to believe in such folly and in many cases people lost their lives because of such beliefs. Women and men were murdered because of their medicine ways, their stories and healings, because of what they believed in and spoke about.

Is our own innocence related?

Now we listen to stories of old, the fantasies and myths acting out some of those stories in the great play of life. Watching in awe on our T.V. screens and looking afresh at how we might gather and learn within community. We are thirsty and hungry for this kind of fantasy and intrigue, of magic and mystery in our culture where technology and science have failed us. They have their benefits, but they cannot possibly give us that sense of magic that we hunger for, not the personal magic that happens inside us. We have created so many wonderful objects, technically advancing our world beyond measure. Yet somewhere deep in our psyche there is a knowing that we are leaving something fundamental behind, advancing ourselves out of a culture that believes in the deeper dream of humanity, that understands there is so much more to our existence than performance, results and financial wealth.

Tolkien gave us the inspirational journey of Bilbo Baggins in The Lord of the Rings and J.K. Rowling gave us the magical experiences of Harry Potter. They are wonderful tales that inspire and remind us of our own imaginations, waking us up to that part of our psyche that has been put too easily to sleep.

We might also recognise that the ways of our imagination are being 'given' to us by outside forces and we are no longer able to manifest this part of us for ourselves, relying on cinema, film, and images thrown at us from the media.

Our own world of imagination and animism is often left as something to be provided for us, by others. The ability to use simple 'tools' to encourage and practice this art has been, in some places, forgotten.

Back in the so-called dark ages, or Middle Ages, our own imagination was relied upon much more. Story-tellers were some of the most important people in the village. Children and adults depended on them, as they wove magical stories of history, fable and myth. Opening up the minds of those who listened, allowing them to create their own pictures and forms, landscapes and imagery, that nourished their minds and fulfilled a need to lessen the hunger of the imagination.

From these stories we sourced great wisdom and an understanding of myth and fairy tale, of history and ancient peoples' lives. We were reminded about where we came from, our heritage and ancestry. It was a way of education, which encouraged learning and new ways to inspire us.

It is possible to reignite some of these old ways through our own culture's rituals and ceremonies. To begin yet again to awaken the Dreamer and learn to trust our dreams, to believe in them and not judge them as something 'unreal'.

Our imagination is key to our own ability to see more, to find the pictures of who we are and to project our desires into the future so that we can manifest from a personal place rather than from what others feel we should know or bring to the world. We need to pay attention to those moments of Spirit, to those 'God moments' in our lives, those synchronicities that make us pay attention a little more to our natural abilities of clairvoyance and 'seeing'.

Empowering our own imagination gives us the freedom to integrate our innocence and curiosity into a functional practice that is as ancient as the rocks of our landscapes. We become the Seer; being able to see clearly, even predict something of our own futures and journeys.

The imagination is recognised as a portal to the spirit worlds and is very much needed in order to follow our shamanic heritage.

In the time of the 'Old Britons', from which I sense my own tribe is connected to in my lineage of wise women, poets, creatives, medicine people and healers; people's belief in nature based gods and goddesses was very clear. Although it is impossible for us to truly know the ancient rites of our lineage here in England and the British Isles, simply because nothing was written down, only passed via storytelling;

we know that people lived their lives with a deep sense of honouring all that was around them. The trees in the forests, the meadow flowers, the elements and clouds in the sky, the stars at night, the light of the fire.

When Christianity arrived, much of their old ways were wiped out, forced to become silent and to go underground, into hiding. Staffs became walking sticks propped at the doorway; rattles were hidden in babies' cradles, old stories and poetry silenced. Our language once called Brythonic was changed to suit the new ways of Christianity and the new order. Romans invaded and this lineage was culled.

We know that our ancestors lived in buildings that were close to nature because they did not want to live separately from nature. They did not want to block the spirit of the land from their homes; they needed to literally live amongst the spirits.

This was their spirituality.

Spirits, dragons, mythical and fairy folk, were all part of the daily spiritual stories and practices. A way to enhance their culture's beliefs, ensuring that their lives were in connection with fables of old. Thus supporting their way of life and their future way of inhabiting the world.

Many rituals were performed, offerings made and songs and prayers spoken.

Their way depended on it.

When the Romans built huge houses and mansions with all their décor and what the Anglo Saxons saw as 'false gods' to deck their halls with, they shut out the very forces that the people of these lands understood to be necessary for their daily survival.

We still build constructions that keep us very much separate from the forces of nature, protecting ourselves from the winds and the rain, turning on our central heating whenever it suits us and not thinking about our consumption of energy. We build our walls thicker, with more substance, in order to shut out the great outdoors. We use air conditioning systems and chop down trees because they spoil our view. What we are doing in our seeking of creature comforts is shutting out the very spirit allies that can give us so much more, if we would listen.

Of course we want comfort and to protect ourselves from the cold and wet. This is natural and it has been possible to find many ways to weave some of the old into the new homes we are building. But still little importance is given to the land.

Instead, we search for something material to give us satisfaction. Do we keep our imaginative world and our fantasy world glued to a box in the living room, replacing the fire's hearth and the visions?

In our own day and age many people are wishing to go back to the land, to live a more natural life with animals, growing their own food and being closer to the elemental forces. It is being recognised as a 'need' in our culture to live in more harmony with Mother Earth and to once again honour her and all of her inhabitants.

We gravitate to indigenous peoples of other lands and countries, somehow putting them on a pedestal, thinking they have got it all right. And in many ways they have, but may lack some of the sophistication we have mastered. There is no 'right' way and we cannot judge ourselves too harshly for wanting to evolve. It is the nature of humankind. But we can find ways to allow the indigenous of our own culture to filter back through our psyches and learn once more to live in harmony with its laws and principles without making it about other cultures.

Do we want to go back to these old times?

We know that is not possible. We must live the way we do and try our best to live with integrity to what we have become and what we do upon this planet. But if we do not learn from our mistakes and we do not at least try to keep some of our heritage alive and honour the traditions of earlier times, then it will be our loss. And not just our loss but also the loss of our beautiful landscapes, its animal and plant life and our inheritors' innocence and birthright.

When we reach into our hearts, connecting to the children that are yet to be born, can we not feel a touch of dread for their souls?

If we do not at least attempt as individuals to pave a better way and instill a way for them to develop their own imagination through their own mind's eye, resourcing them with the ability to connect better with the spirit world, they may feel that sense of loss.

Rather than a generation lost, we support a generation that might have better wisdom, to deal with what seems likely to come.

I feel our ancestors calling to be remembered, for the old ways to have a voice and for us to reignite a sense of spirit in our own homes.

Knowing this need within ourselves, to reclaim the lost parts of our soul and the soul of our own lineage of people, might we invite God/Spirit a little more into our lives?

Can we not help but feel the need to walk on the edge of what is illusion and what is real?

Can we feel the tension of opposing forces and embody the dream to marry our hearts with the yearnings of what it means to truly grow?

We cannot let the dream be merely a fantasy of what could be, but trust that a wider context for the human spirit is around the corner and awaiting its recognition from its people.

And on a basic level, in all of this, we may need to ask for help and guidance from those who will be honest with us, not simply agree or collude with us. Those who recognise what we do not see in ourselves and then accept with humility that some parts of us must change. If we choose to believe then God/Spirit might speak to us through the voices of others, and through their eyes much more will be revealed. We can choose those eyes and ears well, for anyone who will try to justify our feelings, who will try to pacify us and collude with our negative ego, will not be the friend we need.

And our honest approaches and our curiosity will keep embracing it all, bringing new ideas and possibilities into the unfolding. Would this new information fit within our own world?

Would we receive it or not?

And fear and dread may begin to fill our hearts and we recognise the need to make decisions as to whether we take this journey further, walk its path and fulfill its needs. The archetype will begin to show itself more fully, we get hints of it as it begins to tell its tale and choose its own tribe.

We may well need to let go of other aspects of ourselves in order to fulfill this task, to move beyond what society would recognise as agreeable.

Our Sacred Rebel might recognise this and find the need to let go of old ideas that may not work any longer, and we might have a need to separate from it all just for this period of our lives.

How this new way manifests will require all of our attention and focus. And we will need to leave behind what feels old.

* * *

I knew there was more to life and I was going to find it. This meant from a very early age, as young as four, I would pack my suitcase, sometimes with nothing but hats in it. Leaving home, I would walk off into the wide world until I got hungry, lonely or afraid, heading back home again. The bottom of the garden wasn't so far away really, nor was a stroll up the road we lived on, but it sufficed to feel like I was on a mission.

As a teenager these escapades went a bit further, causing worry for my parents and creating havoc for my family.

Once I had a young family myself, my mind would wander away, spacing out, disappearing into worlds of fantasy, and bringing myself back to the demands of little ones. What was I here to do, beyond the normality of everyday living? This was the question I often asked myself.

There was much I needed to release myself from it seemed. I could no longer attempt to be the one I was expected to be. I was making up my own mind about what was the right thing to do, assuring myself I was ok yet somewhere in my heart there was a knowing that I was heading down some very tough journeys that I was not able to escape from.

My rebel nature broke free and yet it forced me into the confines of dysfunction in difficult relationships, trying to manage the mayhem, and be as good a mum as I could be under some duress. Was this part of the story that had needed to unfold?

Recognising that I have felt the need to learn through pain and challenge, even suffering. Ending up in situations over and over that I am sure I could have avoided, but that also became part of its myth.

I recognised the needs that lay beneath this. Partly, I had experienced massive soul loss and could not bring myself back easily unless I was challenged to do so. When my weakness, or the abuse or suffering was so in my face, I could not help but act on it. Talking and problem solving was an analytical spiralling drain that went nowhere, except to find me repeating the same thing over and over again. I would become too lost in the dark, never seeing the light or the potential of possibility, if I would just break free!

I was in denial about my attraction to young abusive men, going back time and time again for the same treatment. Many would say 'What are you doing?', 'Why do you put up with this?' They could see something that I could not. But I was trapped in heartless relationships of my own making, to young men who professed they loved me, but did not know or understand love themselves. I clearly also did not love myself!

We would both be caught in our own patterns with no way of changing them.

I needed something much stronger in order to change this.

Eventually I found it. It took me to the deepest places of my heart and soul, it brought me back to my right size, it tore me limb from limb like a modern day dismemberment journey and I prayed more than I had ever prayed in my life. And with it I met others, those who had walked a similar path, who told familiar tales on how they had managed to change their life around.

I knew I was connecting back to God, recognising my dysfunctions, learning about what would serve me better and discovering what God truly had in store for me. It is an ongoing journey that I expect will take me a lifetime.

I began to recognise that I could change it. Not change it as in one day it is there and one day it isn't, but as a continuing journey and cultivation of deeper awareness, life skills and regular support. My creativity would need to be enhanced, my ability to recognise myself and be self aware would serve the brokenness because then I could do something about it. The gathering of information, the deeper knowing and ultimately the offering would be my gift to others.

My life began to turn around, but not in ways I imagined it would. I had to make many changes in order to free myself from the clutches that did not serve me.

My creativity would be paramount in this, understanding my own creative world, the archetypal qualities and energies I carried. And then embodying what I could learn about their light, rather than constantly dwelling in the shadows.

Our ecstatic nature is the emergence of spirit and our soul's awakening. It creates in us such a high energy where we can appear mad, even crazy. What we do with that typically, in our society, is try and shut it down and medicate it, whatever our drug of choice.

But if we do not, then it might remind us of our own insanity and that will disrupt the status quo. How often do we dance on our streets, sing at the top of our voices in public places when no one else can be heard singing?

How often do we do exactly what feels right, knowing some other will frown upon it?

The spiritual emergence is connected to our own creative voices and dances, our shamanic and indigenous bodies, the ones that are very much at home wherever we are with whatever we are doing.

Our purpose is to find that wild instinctual nature, instead of glorifying the nature of others. We would benefit our own land and heritage, as well as honour the cultures we aspire to by understanding how the emergence of our own spirituality and that of our culture's spirituality, is so necessary and so overlooked.

That wild spiritual nature of inner freedom is often feared in our society with the imagined dangers it might inflict on people, as well as the dangers within society. Too many 'free' people is not great for the economy, the capitalism that rules, or the impact that emotionally fulfilled people would have on pharmaceutical companies. So we can be encouraged to block, to medicate and restrict our natural flows of creativity and joy.

I am always fascinated by our approach to mental health, how we see 'them' and try to rule and control what is out of our own control.

Does it need to be this way and have we worked enough with people who have shown us other ways, another side to what really needs to take place? Sometimes I think not, because we are afraid of change, of trying something new. So we stay as we are, moving in only one direction, blinkered in the face of conduct, regulations and how we are told we/it should be.

A teacher once said to me, 'Go ahead, break that status quo, disrupt what is there, take a risk and create some chaos, after all you are quite a mistress of chaos!' I knew what he meant and noticed where this was easy and where I feared it. In certain places I did not care about where I created or existed in chaos, but in other places, where others had power over me, or whom I had given power too, it would be a little harder to 'rock the boat'. And beneath the surface there was fear.

I was brought up in that nice middle-class family where anger was unspoken, or at least expressing it openly caused a frown. Better to hide it under the shades of an eyebrow, or a sulk somewhere over there in another room.

That seething breath and the sighs of resentment were coiled into our make up, drilled into our senses and forever carried in the gene pool of family heredity.

And I learnt that in order to gain true power and empower myself, I would need to stand up to the authority placed over me and I would need to take those risks to speak out and say 'no' or 'yes' to whatever felt more in line with my heart.

And this is a journey we might all need to take.

This authority was something I once totally accepted, for I knew at the time I needed it. But this same authority I then needed to question, for my own individuation and for my growth and sovereignty to emerge.

We place ourselves under the authority of others in order to learn from them and be able to grow. Then, when that authority is no longer needed and we grow beyond it, we wane and call ourselves back home to our own body, taking back the authority and residing for that time more fully in ourselves. Maybe another authority figure comes along and we attach ourselves to him or her, until that time also wanes as well.

This is healthy for a time. We need to give the authority to those we wish to learn and grow from. It means I give them the permission to call me on my bullshit and to make suggestions to do things differently, or to give me different perspectives on circumstances or behaviours. This is all normal. We might need that transference for a while as we learn to grow up. If those we give our authority to are healthy in their ability to lead and support and they have looked a long way into their own history, then we can be in good hands.

If they share from their experience and encourage us to find our way without inflicting 'their way' on us or making demands on us, then we can be sure we are learning to grow without any kind of countertransference, which would mean that they were starting to respond to us like our parents for example, or becoming needy of us. The healthy leader, the one holding that authority, will spot this happening and will be able to correct where necessary. It is then appropriate for a time to allow the transference of the individual, until it is time to let it go.

However, if we do not allow the eventual waning of authority to happen but remain clinging like a needy child to that parent figure, chances are we will fall into old patterns and succumb to the stories that keep us small without a voice.

Firstly, we must identify the pattern that plays through us and then try to find a different way. Those of us with wounds so deep they have caused us great humiliation and suffering, will find it much harder to let go of authority, returning time and time again, addicted to the very thing that is making us small or even sick! Our actions will perpetuate these wounds and we will remain stuck in our own story.

But our soul purpose begins to land, shaking up the spiritual within us. It is an inevitable consequence of life at some point, we cannot bear to remain the same.

This can come as a mighty force, shaking us up and creating havoc in its midst. We may find ourselves speaking out in ways we have never done before. We may act in ways that rock the boat on those treacherous waves, we may tug at the framework of what has been familiar and destroy connections that served us partially well.

Spiritual emergence will take its toll. It must wake us up fully and demand our fullest attention. We may feel like things are going horribly wrong, where words pour from our mouths that we have never heard before and friendships become fragmented. Families may become disrupted and our careers, our work or whatever else has held value in our lives is left in disarray. Life is falling apart and things must change. It is a confusing time and again we feel we are going mad!

We are afraid of the future, it is unstable and we have no idea what direction we are going in. Spirit rattles our bones and speaks to us in many tongues. It empties us out and loosens our grip on normality. Thrown open upon the shores of life we must beg spirit to take us, to do with us its will. We are in service and we find ourselves begging to be taken and moved through.

There is no other way but through, else we become tormented by dreams and fall over and over again into a pit of despair.

At this point many people will be seen as having temporary breakdowns, given medication to calm them down, even sectioned in extreme cases. Families will simply not know any other way to deal with this so-called 'problem'.

But if we are aware, with enough resources, we will find our way through, being kind to ourselves and seeking the help that we know is necessary. Time is a beautiful healer, as is self-care and nurturing.

This is a time for dreams to come through, for voices to be heard and taken seriously. It is a time to honour the ancestors of our lineage and begin to focus on the healing that may need to come through our bodies to help serve them. Then, any previous 'spiritual sickness' that was not given appropriate attention has the opportunity to end in the here and now, so we no longer need to carry the wounds of our ancestors.

Voices begin to be heard, hearts express what needs to be expressed and a deep listening emerges. The psyche's disturbance is taken seriously. The soul is waking up and is entering our body, whether it is cathartic, or a simple awakening to understanding there is more to our life.

What do we do with this?

We need to find others who will take this seriously and not go to the people who will try and make us return to our old self, telling us they do not like who we have become, that they want the one who was familiar to them to be here. They are simply not ready for our growth and our full experience of life.

Those people who will force us towards medication or the psychiatrist's chair may not be the ones who will support our spiritual growth. They will not encourage the particular song we need to sing, the music we need to play or the path we feel we must follow. They will not encourage us to re-wild ourselves with nature and write the poetry that comes from deep in the cells of our body.

This is not to say that there aren't exceptions and every person and situation must be taken accordingly and appropriately into consideration.

But from my own experience I know I have needed a guide to enable some level of soul retrieval to begin. Someone who comes very well recommended, who has a strong sense of vision as well as good experience. They must be walking their own path and have undergone much of their own healing and teaching for many years. They can support the one who is dreaming their soul through and understand the need for the 'dark night of the soul'. They are not afraid of what they will see. They are spiritual midwives and have witnessed many birthings before.

Most of all, they have their own strong connection to their God or Spirit, they know this journey and they know how to enter into those depths. And especially, they know how to bring themselves back.

For we cannot support anyone to visit a place we cannot ourselves return from.

And this work we must do, for the sake of all of our souls and the re-membering that needs to happen. Seeking out others on a similar path will be beneficial, as will spending much time alone if we feel able to, if it is safe for us to do so. There we can visit loneliness and speak to the self that has found its way to this gateway.

Meeting loneliness will take us deep into our psyche to dig in the depths of our wounds, to sort through the fears and the sorrows, to meet anger face to face – not the anger of others but the anger we hold. We will need time alone, time to meet ourselves, to find out a little more about ourselves and our relationship to this one.

Too long in the loneliness will not serve, for that is punishment. We need others, we need connection and we need the mirror of our neighbours to reflect more about ourselves. This is how we begin to identify who we are.

A Wretched Landscape

Concrete misshapen paving slab after slab
Nowhere to go but down, no real growth
Just trodden down into shadow and gutter
No place for creature but tamed, poisoned or maimed
What nature
Unveiled when hidden and timeless yet knowing
she is here
In the cursed wretchedness of a landscape barren with body
after body of lifeless despair
Filth beyond filth and not the sort that plays
with puddles
makes mud and lines footprints
with where we have been
But underneath that trodden down cardboard cut out plastic
rubbish bag collected one day but forgotten too soon
Homeless wreckage hunger for companion, still emerges
sweetness and understanding of a ghost that left a
home too many moons ago
Lost in a land of unknown multitudes of belly aches
and doctors bills
No time to watch the arena of youth passing by and
not notice that it's changing beyond repair
Beyond repair if we speak and dare, just dare to be
the spoken voice of a game gone wrong
No hope to belong

Not to belong but master the obsession
If possible if one can
If that risk be undone and life prevails
If life
And if……

My interests began to unfold around the journey of soul and particularly the soul's purpose through the human body. I studied and recalled my own life. Remembering the thoughts and feelings I had as a child. Writing my books, poetry and stories, exploring the dance, animals, and my connection to nature and creativity. I also became fascinated with other cultures and how they would interpret the very thing that had captured my own curiosity.

In tribal communities when a baby is born, its elders would watch to see what that child would become drawn to, what his or her interests were, his or her callings. And they would support whatever that was, knowing that the child had inherited its own soul's call and was beginning to live it out. Attracting to him or her the very things and way of life needed for his/her potential and growth. The elders were so much closer to the new born innocent soul, being at the end of their life journey and the baby at the beginning of hers.

In Dagara life, the child's early years are spent with the grandparents. The grandparents and the grandchild have a shared connection that is very much alive with the spirit worlds. They are so much closer to birth and death. The parents are not there with them in that closeness. The grandparents are awake to the messages they can receive from the grandchild, information that the child can bring back to their community and also what they might need for the journey they are soon to take. They will need to gather that information before the child forgets it themselves, just as their parents have done.

We can see this in many cultures where the grandparents have a special bond with the newborn.

But in more modern societies, unless we are truly awake, we have lost that way of 'seeing' the soul and its contract with God/Spirit, therefore we dismiss the awakenings that happen to us over time and through our lives. We often give them no relevance.

We have forgotten the art of supporting the soul to inhabit the human body, to marry soul and ego and form the allegiance needed for the continued growth and purpose of the soul's life on earth.

Our forefathers and foremothers could teach us this if we were willing to step back into the ancestral lineage of our culture, remember some of its story-telling, artistry and poetry. Listening, looking for the signs and remembering a people who lived simply and in congruence with the natural world around them. Of course it was not always ideal and we cannot return to the old ways, but there are old wives' tales that rumble in the bones of our memory. There is wisdom right at the back of our minds, a calling from the cellular stories we carry and a knowing and a spiritual awakening every time we get close to the truth.

So CAN we 'dream ourselves awake?'

When there is a need to follow an awakening, it is as if part of us has been missing and is being recalled. At that time we can feel alone, we can lose a sense of our own identity. Then we can get a sense of having lost our way and nothing will work but a quick fix medicated spur of ingredients, that will then plumet us even lower into the darkest of nights.

What is often missing is our connection to Spirit, to God, to community, our connection with others. Whatever it is to us that says, 'I am not alone'. It is then when we must venture outwards, into the unknown, into the many different kinds of forests that beckon our call.

I had an innate understanding that we each had a purpose in our lives and it was up to us to take a journey to find out what that was. The hero's journey fascinated me.

I prayed a lot to God and asked questions about what I was supposed to be doing. I would imagine myself older and try to understand that whatever happened to me, God must want it to be that way, but I had to play my part. I didn't know what that part was and I had many failures along the way. There were times I did not seek guidance and persevered on my own, which was not the best way to be by any means. My own will power can be a mixture of confusion, manipulation, forcefulness and arrogance.

Something to keep in check!

Still, I had a very expansive mind, wanting to stretch it and understand what was beyond the parameters of my small world. I was always deep in thought, very serious and in many ways – isolated.

My curiosity needed to know more.

* * *

We have all worn the Sovereign's golden crown in that black rucksack on our backs. We have left home, finding our way through a rugged landscape of unfamiliar terrains. Not knowing where we should be, we still went on that journey. It was like a hand on our back, edging us forward. We didn't dare look back because if we did we would possibly find out too soon and the path would not then be taken.

We must walk that path if we are to discover the story, for it is in the repetitive patterns and the gathering of totems where we become aware of signs that need to be taken notice of.

* * *

Many years ago I created a ritual, something that preceded the eventual outcome of that process. For years it was growing inside me, being digested, waiting for the right time to emerge and meet with its fruition. Only after those years did it truly play itself out in my life as many of our rituals do, sometimes taking a day or two, sometimes years!

I was preparing for my graduation within the organisation I had studied in for some years. I was now finding my own way in the world and creating my own offering.

Many great, great grandmothers had created theirs before me and now it was my turn, with what felt like their ancestral support at my back.

There on one of those occasions was my little black suitcase, sitting in the corner of my bedroom which beckoned to me, I imagined packing it and leaving home. On that one occasion, filling it with hats, a hat for every occasion. But where was the golden crown?

I knew it was possible that once I graduated I would again take my bag, not the same black suitcase of course, but a bag never-the-less. It would be packed this time with my own purpose and soul's offering, my own tools. I would step fully away, without looking back at the organisation I had been part of for many years.

I did not doubt this.

But I was not certain at all when this time would be, despite the fact that at that time I had a very strong pull to leave! I would need to wait, head into the ceremony and see what unfolded. What felt right at that time is what I would follow. Maybe the ceremony was going to show me!

So I sang my way into ceremony, with around thirty other women, each being with their own particular craft, their own weaving, sewing, and writing and playing of instruments – every woman with a red ribbon around their wrists. These ribbons represented our own blood, wherever we were in our menstrual cycle.

And as we sang, those who were in the perimenopausal time of their life held up their arms to create a passageway. And the elders of our group, those who had been through that gateway of menopause took the ribbons from their wrists and placed them into the central cauldron. They turned and made their way through the passage of perimenopausal women and faced back at us in line.

I stirred the cauldron with my own stick, the red knowledge of blood. And taking off my own ribbon I walked through that line of women, meeting each elder as our eyes and hearts connected.

And there in the background sat the representative of Death. Our true elder, the one we must all become one day; our greatest teacher in life.

Sitting with my friend who played the role of Death, she blew upon my throat. We spoke a few words, sitting together, listening and contemplating.

And then to my amazement I realised I had forgotten the packed bag, the one I was meant to bring with me, the one of my own medicine, the one I was meant to leave with! I whispered to Death, 'I cannot be ready to leave'. Is this what was to make the final decision?

I knew then that I could not leave yet, I simply wasn't ready. Despite being uncomfortable in this organisation, I could not tear myself away. I may never fully know the reason why, the addiction was strong, something else needed to happen and right now I did not know what it was. One thing I learnt was that it would happen. But it would happen in God's time and not in my time. For that day I would need to be patient, because I could not control it.

Back to that ritual, I was becoming one with the elder women, knowing my own menopause was established, standing in their company, my ritual was nearly complete.

I called my guardians to be present and held my staff in hand. Speaking my truth, honouring the journey, I shared why I was there for that time.

Stepping through the hoop of recognition, I was seen and I held the graduation torch in my heart.

And then there came a time, some months later, when the path became clearer and it truly was time to leave. This I absolutely knew for I was living in that God time, I was surrendering to the will of Spirit and my intention was clear. I held the beginnings of my own Medicine Wheel, the Wheel Of Soul's Return, in my heart, and it was becoming known to me.

Some months later I made the intention to offer my swan song to a group of women, where they would gather together under my guidance and create their own medicine bags.

And there again was the same woman, who played and represented Death at my last ritual. She stood at my side throughout that time, and supported my decision to be leaving the organisation, as she made her offer in service to the work that I was holding.

I gathered with those forty women, offering to them what I knew of my own medicine. And took them through a process of creating their bags, stitching and sewing into the cloth and materials, singing their own songs into those threads and stitches, into that cloth. The bag showing them, inside and outside, who they really were and what the path was that they would follow.

This work, completed and offered to others, marked the medicine of my own calling. The offering of my soul's journey. I became free to follow what I truly needed. To share my own medicine with others and allow the body of work that had been the story of my life to come into its own wisdom field.

I was no longer connected to the organisation that though trained me, had also held me in place. And that in some ways, many had told me, had been keeping me small. That bursting out was the energy that was my own swan opening her wings and letting them know, I am free to do as I please, as I need and to allow my God/Spirit to be the only authority in my life.

I began to stir my own cauldron of medicine, to see the potential of my soul's purpose.

And then that gateway opened up and I could be totally true to myself and who I really was. There was nothing to run away from because I could not leave myself.

I needed to grow into my own Sovereign and take responsibility for the work that is God's work, that is the potential I was born with and knowing what that is, is only for my own soul to truly know. For this offering is a God-conscious one, not a self-conscious or a subconscious one but fully and spiritually conscious because it does not come from a place of ego. Yet ego is its servant.

Notes

Apprenticing to Our Truth

Learning about who we are and what we are here to do means that we must become the Apprentice to our own life story. There are many other things we could apprentice to, but this one must be at the core if we are to truly know our vocations.

We need to know our journey, our patterns, our habits, the things that we love, what we feel passionate about and what has called to us, asking for our interest . We also need to know what has put us more in touch with our soul, to understand some of the suffering and where we ourselves have created disturbances.

We must understand our life, turn some of the old stones over, see what lurks inside and unveil the darkened corners. This way we get to see more of ourselves and we begin to know what is ours to bring more of to the world.

We can see what we have learnt from experiences and from our strengths to become a better human and to reclaim what has been lost. We get to acknowledge where we have gone wrong and where we have acted on our will power and nothing more. We see the craziness of our life and how we have come to clear the path and make good of what has ailed us.

And then we begin to bring through the amazing gifts that become uncovered, that are woven together across the repetitions and patterns of the tapestry of our life story.

What have we grown with?

For me, my curiosity lies mostly around the support of innocence. Whether it be a newborn, a child, an animal, a small seedling, the beginning of a dance, or the first words on a page. Each story unfolding touches me and I find myself fascinated with its fragility and new beginning in life.

I'm aware of my protective spirit, the animal nurturer in me. I hold a deep caring and that protectiveness has never left me. I have a love of little ones, of new growth, wherever that is. My mothering, my grandchildren, it all fascinates me. I love planting seeds and watching them grow and I am drawn, always, to the excitement of new beginnings, observing and supporting whatever it is.

It might be the beginnings of a project, the artist's first moments as a painting begins to appear, or the first moments as we dream in a new idea. The excitement that is revealed to us at that time and the curiosity that unfolds.

I love beginnings.

I've spent my life giving attention to this very thing, looking at various models of personal development, spiritual practices and therapeutic growth, finding that 'return to innocence' within each one and how it might need support.

Each has given me something to grasp onto and to look a little deeper at myself, possibly in a new way each time. But it has only been much later on in life that I really began to see who I had become. Because the way it seemed to me, was that I had had to live my life in order to see what it was really about. I had to get to at least my fifties in order to understand the path I had walked and what God had intended for me. What was it that was made known at my own beginning and what was this fascination for innocence and vulnerability?

My own excitement with this led me to a creative path that enforced my own innocent, curious nature to wake up again and begin to create it into a form I could share with others.

I love divination and allowing something to guide me, something that is outside myself. Laying the cards on the table, I feel a trust in what I will be shown.

I hear a comrade speaking about something that I am trying to deal with in my own life, I hear that experience and maybe I am touched by it because I get an insight into what I am looking for, or struggling with.

I gain hope.

I walk in nature and I see the colours and feel the textures of this landscape and I am reminded of my own true nature, where I am from and where I will inevitably return. I pick up a stone, of a particular shape, and it speaks to me, maybe reminding me of a story held long ago.

I watch a play, or a film, I read a book of another's tale, I witness art and I am moved in some way unexpectedly because it reached into a part of my own journey of soul that reminded me where I was going.

I feel that awakening moment.

In these and so much more, I witness the journey that is mine and I am guided to do better, to strive for less or to accept my life as it is. I am touched in my heart and reminded of my vulnerability as well as my strengths.

And a map was created, a map I could honestly call 'my life,' that showed me so many of my own patterns, my habits, my beliefs and what I had learnt as a child and now led me to be the adult I had become. It was full of experiences that somehow felt universal and connected to others around me.

Part of this map showed me some of my flaws, my dysfunctions and the losses that I have endowed on myself. I would see and understand my own abdication of sovereignty, my shadow-self. Knowing that in order to grow, we must all explore what lies in the shadows and attempt at least to unravel some of the hurts and angers that have accumulated throughout our life.

I must ask myself why I am angry and why I might be full of fear. Why might I find authority difficult and why might my voice at times be left unheard?

All of these must be examined closely if I am to be free and if I am to do no harm to others.

I had always expected that at some point I would receive my own particular work and get to know it more fully, to then be able to offer it to others, but I realised eventually that all I truly had to offer to others was in fact my experience, my strengths and what I had lived through myself. How else could I pass on a legacy that was in any way useful?

To me it seems important to leave something behind, even a few words that could possibly support others on this journey through life. I am simply a channel for God's love and it is that love that makes this real for me. I have so appreciated what others have left in service for us now, those Seer's who have known a little of our future, who have spelt things out for us. Whether we listen or not, they still honoured the future lineages and children with their wisdom and understanding.

* * *

As I witnessed the map of the journey I had lived through and began to see its potential, I saw it as a tree of life, but in a way that each of my own experiences fitted into its segments. It was a diagram of what I would call the 'soul's return' and was linked to an ancient system, a kabbalah, a rite of passage, a hero's journey. A system written a million times over, not specifically mine but a link to many, to the hearts and lives of those who came before me and to those who come after me.

Through my own life story, I discovered different stages of the soul's return, the marking and making of each stage, deepening the process and unveiling more of who I was and the potential of this map for others.

The stages took me into nine gateways, which can be seen on the cards and in the Wheel.

There are nine Dwellings. I gave them the names from the many workshops I had held over all those years of sharing the dance. I found it helped to visualise each of those dwellings as pieces of deep work that the soul could be birthed through.

I began noticing a certain archetypal quality for each one, a symbolic tool and a resource that I felt served this deep work. They each beckoned to me, to grow with their emotional intelligence, offering a stronger sense of empowerment.

Knowing too that each stage would be different for each individual, we are not the same. But in learning about this, we would share with each other, finding an even richer human landscape to explore.

For there are many landscapes of the mind, heart and body territory.

Would we leave things out?

There is much work to do. For example, are we still living out some of our dramas, the small ones and the greater ones? Who have we hurt along the way and what can we now do to make amends for some of that? What was not our fault as youngsters that we have had to find a way to heal from, or to forgive? So often we can imagine the wrongs we have done and yet we were simply victims of another's crimes or dysfunctions. When we discover that, then there is a great weight that falls from our shoulders. The shame and guilt are diminished and we can be free from the grip of that sickness.

It is like a purging of the old, cleaning our psyche, from the inside. Ensuring we are no longer living out the wounds and malfunctions of previous years.

This would be the work needed in the first trimester of the Wheel, to get to know our story as that innocent one.

I needed to study, to be the apprentice of this journey, to read stories, to get feedback and listen to how others perceived the work. I would need to take advice from those I trusted, from those I felt could be totally honest with me and reflect back any misgivings or doubts, even fears. Everything would have a place to be heard. I could not do this by myself.

The dance continued and gradually I began to learn about this offering in depth, the way I wanted to work with it, the way I would tell its story with its poetry and prose.

I gradually began to piece my own life back together, to find out who I really was as I included this new offering.

* * *

I learnt that I abandoned my own needs for a while, which is quite easy for us to do, particularly as parents, after many challenges within relationships and generally living my life under difficult circumstances. I began to grow through a deep and introspective time. And with the dance, I began to witness myself more closely, to understand the path I was on and to follow what became the most important aspects of what I was here to do.

My passion then was spelt out to me in the making of the Wheel, and it was time to put it into action!

Notes

Artisan – The lover of life

As an Artisan, I see what is reflected back to me: the art, the creativity and who I become when I witness this.

What will my hands create, what song might I sing, what poetry will my lips unfold? For there are so many ways to be the artist; the speaker, the writer, the musician, the architect, the gardener and sower of seeds, whatever the art, whatever the calling.

I am a lover of all that is beautiful, my eyes seek out that beauty in every part of my life. And not just what the eye beholds as beauty, but the touch, the smells, the sensations that warm my heart. And not just the beauty in what is typically beautiful, I see beauty in the dark, in the shadow, in what lurks in the background, hiding from view.

Afraid to be seen, beauty can hide under locks of hair. It can hide in a statement or words from a darkened character, heavy with the stench of booze lurking on the corner of the street. Somehow his smile or his words speak a moment of kindness and longing. This is the grit and the poetry of life, the frame of a story, a soul lost in the undercurrents, that very few can comprehend or understand.

The girl whose art has failed time and time again, whose broken heart has left her in a sorry state of bewilderment. Still she paints on and creates from the pain of despair.

There is beauty in the hunger of the one who has never been loved, who reaches for that one moment in time for connection, for a creative piece that longs to be shown to the world, and through all the longing is then met – yet the hand pulls away for fear of the unknown.

My heart moves and I write the poetry that inspires that broken heart to reach out once more, to become the lover of one's own art and embrace its calling.

The singer and songwriter, who cannot help but sing from the heart, yet falls on deaf ears as our culture rushes by. No time to listen, to feel, to soak in the timeless harmonies that flow effortlessly, yet have been worked so hard at to improve and make perfect.

Yes, art comes in so many forms; the lover's touch put into the creative purpose and we are held for a moment as there is no knowing, as yet, what that art will become.

I myself was no perfect artist. I loved to draw and paint and make things with my fingers, but for me it was always the words and the poetry, the creation of a book that could, if I was lucky, fall into many hands.

And then it was the dance that could create so many living sculptures and shapes, so much choreography that came only from the present moment, no planning or working out the posture or the performance. And the actress and lover of improvisational theatre that needed total presence and simply a saying of 'yes' to whatever was unfolding. I also love to create a beautiful home and garden, finding every item placed in the perfect place for my eye to see; the flowers, the shapes of borders, the flow of the pathways.

The artist lives in all of us, if we allow it, if we give it permission to really live.

But will we?

Where did it come from? What were its origins?

Could it have been from way, way back in our ancestry? A gift that has come through the ages and our inheritance that has merged with its spirit, supporting us to carry on its talent, its medicine?

My mother was not allowed the path of the artist, for her father deemed it unsuitable for a woman of her age and she was lost in a world of serving others, of being the secretary for men's business, to grow the business to market their shares. Her place in the artists' school was simply not allowed, despite having been granted a scholarship by those who could see her talents. She must surely have lived with that undying resentment towards her family, wishing her life away for a moment of that recognition.

The dreaming artist's body holds many tales. It can give us the courage to be an ambassador for the spiritual world and a necessary warrior for the times we live in today.

WILL we dream ourselves awake?

Will we take up the call to arms with our paintbrushes and instruments? Will we call again to the spirit of the dance and write the poetry that sits in our hearts? Warriors of the creative life force – is this the tool to bring home our soul? To inhabit our bodies without need for materialistic wealth, without need for power over others, without need for fame and fortune?

For the wealth of this alone is enough and it is that, that we have forgotten. It is that, that will allow us to live more fully, to combat the depression of our ancestral lineage. It is that, that reminds us of the free dancer and the life force in our veins.

We are all creative, we were born that way, we came to life that way amidst our mother's blood and artistry. The singing wailing voice of protest and that love and blessing, welcoming us into the life we were to lead. We are known to God, to Spirit, to have that voice, to be remembered as our true and divine nature.

Dare we take it into the life stream now and remember it fully?

We know that every culture has its own creative, indigenous memory. It lies within the rocks and the stone people. It flows through the winds of time in the tops of our trees, rustling the leaves, saying listen to our song. It flickers, each flame, one at a time, as the fire reminds us of the creative source.

Man walked and created in the landscape wherever we dwell. Wisdom was known and yet in some parts wiped out; language, rituals and ceremonies forbidden and forgotten.

Some cultures are fortunate enough to remember theirs, to still be able to adopt their heritage.

Even if it has been suppressed, segregated and abused, sometimes to the point of near extinction, it is still recognisable in some way. In some cultures it has been forced out of existence and is barely recognisable, so it seeps out from the corners of humanity, peering out from behind closed doors and through hair that covers the eyes.

'I am here, I am waiting to be seen and recognised, my song is waiting to be sung.'

Notes

Parenthood as Guardian of The Soul

As parents we want what is best for our children and as they grow, if we are not careful, that can manifest as control and manipulation, trying to keep them safe so that we do not feel the discomfort and pain that their stepping into the world can bring. There is of course much to fear.

Being a mother myself, I learned that I had made many mistakes and I needed to learn about them and put them right.

I am sorry for the mistakes I made in my children's upbringing, but I also held a trust in them to find their own way and make their own decisions in life. I didn't always find it an easy thing to learn or do, but there was an innate understanding in me that they were not there for me to control, or for me to live my life through theirs! But it is their life, their choice and they must learn from their own challenges and their own mistakes and it is the way of their own soul's purpose and who am I to deny them that?

What happens when we (or anyone else) find our soul purpose? When that calling becomes so utterly obvious and we know we can no longer resist. When we know that the reason for us being here on this planet is clear.

If a 'healer' receives the calling, it cannot easily be refused. But that one will need to heal themselves first and take time out of normal society and mainstream activities in order to give attention to and focus on their tasks. This is not always what is wanted and many will try and divert the call and they will not adhere to the calling with the right spirit or intention.

Whatever the call, whether to become a healer or to find one's true purpose in many other forms, it is possible that we meet with fear, anxiety and the need to have others' approval, thus making the timing of our approach a crucial part of the process.

In native and traditional, indigenous teachings, the soul's purpose is welcomed and honoured as soon as it is witnessed. Youngsters are given encouragement and are challenged appropriately to master their art and to fulfil their potential. If a young 'healer to be' is noticed, he/she is taken under the wing of an elder and nurtured carefully, he/she is given the appropriate guidance and teachings. In our western society, the calling expressed by a youth can be frowned upon, not taken seriously and discouraged, as if it is not important enough and some other path is.

So when youngsters tell us what they know to be their path, their career, their learning path, how will we meet it?

Can we give a total 'yes' to what they know is right for them and trust their decisions, even if it changes later on, or must we inflict our own desires, wishes and ultimately our own needs on their growth? If we become aware of a youngster displaying an unfamiliar attitude, a strange 'out of the ordinary' way of behaving in our 'normal' society, what do we do?

From what I have witnessed and experienced, we do our utmost to bring that youngster to normality, trying to educate them to 'fit in' and not be different from their peers. Thus many children are medicated, sent to 'special' schools, labelled as misfits and discouraged from their purpose.

When we discover a true path for ourselves and know the importance of this in our lives, can we stand strong in the face of adversity and believe enough in ourselves to speak out and open our hearts to our true nature? Can we learn to recognise this in our children, without being scared that they will be different?

What does it take to honour the soul and include the passions of our soul purposes as the true growth of potential?

In a talk I gave recently on soul retrieval, I spoke about how I home-schooled my children for some of their childhoods. Not all, but some of the time. I had not planned on talking about the upbringing of my children or to share information about my choice of homeschooling or going to school, it just happened that way.

However, as I spoke, I found this topic coming quite spontaneously and spoke very much 'in the moment'. It was then that I realised, I had an experience that was in fact very useful to others, and that I had learnt much from the motherhood homeschooling experience.

One woman wrote to me saying, 'I remember you sharing about your daughter dressing in shell suits and bling as a teenager and you realised that your children had to push against you, even though you were flexible and permissive in some ways, perhaps more than others. So the fact that you were an earth mother meant she had to become the opposite to be able to explore her own identity. I have since shared this idea with others, that our children actually need to push and rebel against us, that in fact we should expect it. It was an important teaching for me.'

Seeing my children, now full-grown, I was able to see what had worked well and what had not worked so well in their education as well as their necessary rebelling.

I could share some of the challenges, some of the benefits. I could look back on our lives together and see what had been learnt. Of course, there were moments that I didn't do it well and made mistakes, and there were times when my children had a wonderful time and experienced things they would never have experienced otherwise. They will obviously have their own stories to tell about how it was for them but what I see in them today is as a result of their collective experiences and of their own soul contracts to be here on the earth at this time.

They mainly grew up in a rural setting, having the freedom to wander and play, to have animals both small and large and to create as they needed to. In some ways they were very fortunate with this and in some ways they missed out on cultural aspects of city life. But later, they made up for any lack and were quite able to fit into both worlds. A bit like me going from city and factory to horse riding and all my other outdoor nature-experiences.

In the first year of having a school aged child, I followed my mother's opinions for a while. The local village school was what was needed. But after a while, I did not like what I saw or felt, so I looked into the Steiner Kindergarten which was much more in keeping with my own attitudes and beliefs around education. They had less pressure on them to learn to read and write very early on. My own experience of that age probably had something to do with that decision! I also liked how creative they were in the Steiner school and how they encouraged children to play.

Once too old for kindergarten and there being no first year class there in those days, I looked at the first year of the local primary school. I was not so keen on the schooling system at all, but I recognised the need for them to be with friends and peer group. They also desired this and so it was decided.

Observing the attendance of school being a difficult one, it was not the happiest of experiences for them. We persisted for some years, but in time a different choice needed to be made.

I chose home-schooling and they agreed. It worked well and our focus was more on creativity with art, music, play, connection to nature and animals.

I learnt a lot about innocence from this. How children developed their own needs and hobbies, how they found their way, following what I would now call a soul purpose, to see why they truly are here to offer what they offer. It was up to me to guide that path, to encourage and to simply say 'yes' to all they turned their hand to.

I allowed my children to make their own decisions about school, whether they went or not. From what I now know about homeschooling it was easier then, regards the education system. It worked for us at times and at other times they went to school when they were at ease with it.

He said he could not understand why
the teachers spoke to him the way they did,
why they did not have conversations
and allow him an opinion?

He came home complaining that he wasn't
allowed to knit with the girls and had to play
football with boys. He could do that with
his brothers anyday!

He didn't like not being able to finish a project,
there was too little time. Always another subject,
then another...

She was bored with the lack of creativity.
'Why can't I just paint what I want?'.

Conversations like that persuaded me that the decision to homeschool was a better idea, for that time.

It was hard work for me, I needed space myself, but to see my youngsters learning and growing together was so worth it.

There was much we might have missed out on, if it had not been that way and so easy for their true passions not to have been spotted if they were scooped up into the everyday, daily routines of school life. Their individuality was prominent, it was always very clear to me, even the subtleties.

So it was easy to encourage them to follow their own passions.

To this day I can see how each one has developed that path, their soul purpose, to the level it needs to be today. Nature has been a calling, along with creativity, music, parenting, film making, gardening and all manner of interesting assignments and projects.

Who knows how it will inform their future, but I can see the thread weaving its way through their lives and I am so proud to witness them along that path.

I am now witness to all my now adult children, following their path, in a way that only they can decide upon. It is not my place to insist or to sculpt and make things happen that I think should happen. It is not my life to control and force decisions upon so that I might be more comfortable. 'If only' I used to think 'that schools could see it that way too.' If only my parents and society could begin to understand that we are all here with our own purpose that needs to be honoured. It is not always easy and it does not necessarily fall into our lap, but gentle perseverance and showing up in the right moments is a good starting point.

We need to work for our purpose, and to remember the contract we made before we were born. That way we grow into our soul's calling, as it awakens in us, and we give it our time, patience, perseverance, focus and discipline. Resting into each stage in order for it to find its own way.

Motherhood and Fatherhood is a time of allowing, of saying 'yes' to those we gave birth to. We can be extremely pressured into doing things the way that society insists we do them, that there is a 'right' way of bringing your baby up, as though we can't be trusted to figure it out for ourselves.

How might we learn to read the signals from our own child, just as our foremothers did, recognising those baby signals and acting accordingly?

'Don't spoil that child by giving in too soon, it will be the ruin of him or her.' Boundaries yes, but the authorities choose to rule over us. As a parent and someone who instinctively knows to allow a child to follow their own instincts and to trust them enough, means they find their own self-esteem.

As a mother or father this then leads to further understanding of what is best for the young child. And there comes a time to let go that bit more, so they can begin to learn about themselves and the world around them.

All of my children have made so-called mistakes and as a mother it was my role to allow them to, because they needed to learn how to rectify them themselves, not to be scolded continuously by me.

Can this be a better way?

And so I went on being pulled by my heartstrings, learning over and over to step back and allow them their mistakes and their challenges, so that they would learn from life's lessons and they would grow and excel beyond the needy child and I the overpowering mother!

I trusted the greater scheme of things and despite stepping back being agonising at times, I saw what the great universe of life had in store for them. In this place I become a guardian, creating a space for their growth. And once they came of age, then it would be my job to let them go.

Of course, the father too must create protection, safety and good teachings, if he can. And we must all do our best to allow that soul its place on the earth and in community, no matter what it brings to the table. I cannot speak or write from the father's perspective of course.

Even if the child brings the most ordinary of offerings, even if he must work in a factory and she becomes a cleaner for others, there is nothing that is not worthwhile. The most important thing is to simply be the best cleaner or best factory worker that they can possibly be. We cannot judge them for this, we cannot want that high-powered job for them, or desire a high net salary simply because it would give them perceptively more security. It is not the way of the soul, to be needed or to fit to another's plan.

The children we bring up today are the leaders of our future. How we birth them, support them and educate them truly matters if we are to see a world changed from the old and tired paradigms, worn out structures and outdated systems that no longer serve.

We as mothers and fathers can change our own ways of controlling and disciplining our children by honouring their choices, trusting them to know who they are and who they wish to be in the world.

We cannot always make decisions for them, therefore we must 'let go' at appropriate times to allow them their own growth with their soul's purpose.

The Thespian's Call to the Shapeshifter

And the Thespian would step out with his or her art, a little further onto the stage of life, embracing the future with open arms, 'Here is what I have for all to see. I will find the cloak and fabric of my own soul; it will show itself as I reveal it more.'

I believe that the soul is our natural essence, our inner dancer, our innate wisdom. And life is the teacher, the gift of experiences. So there is a need for us to make space for this essence to inhabit us, to fill us and become us.

The teachings come in many forms, through life's challenges, through dark nights, through the inspirational and God moments. Through heart awakenings and connections with others, whatever is presented to us along the way.

When on that journey to heal some of the old stories, the parts of us that no longer serve a purpose are released, we find new actions to replace the old, adopting the shape-shifter and changing what we understand to be ours to change.

If you can imagine that once we are much clearer in ourselves, with less attachment to the past, we can become that empty or semi-empty vessel that spirit/energy can pass through more easily like a channel. Then you can imagine this shapeshifter state, a meditation, a silence that flows simply as energy, from all that is around us and above us. Through the mind and the heart, the body is like a musical instrument, a flute, an empty space. The calling finds its way. We shapeshift into the one who calls through us.

It means an emptiness of story, much clearing is being done. We are freer from past restrictions and judgements about ourselves, we have had enough spiritual awakenings to meet our calling, we are embracing the possibility of a new kind of freedom and our lives have become much richer in spirit and in joy. What is it that will flow through us and what shape will we become?

If we are keen to follow this journey and discover more, and dance has become a gateway for this, then we might enter into the ecstatic nature of the dance, often coming far and wide to be together and creating community. We might recognise that this is a route to our healing because we must include body, heart and mind to find that deeper connection to spirit. It cannot only be done by thinking and intellectualising.

As we get to find our community, our tribe of people, we develop the safety between us and it deepens. Trust is magnified and becomes palpable in the field, there comes a time where we can immerse ourselves deeper into our personal and collective process. Embarking on the story of our life and the way we have lived, looking at who we have become and addressing some of our past.

What has led us to our own particular suffering and some of the challenges we have faced?

True healing happens when we change our actions. For many, the constant sharing and regurgitation of a story from our past will only support the victim in us. The dramas will be an endless form of entertainment and the addiction to tell it and grow it will deepen. This will not serve us and only adrenalise our state of being.

And we cannot allow the victim to have more power than it already has. The way to heal is to act differently, to ensure the old behaviours are no longer happening in any form. It is the work of our own apprentice archetype, studying our life story, that discovers the old repetitive patterns, what is useful and what is old!

It is the new action that heals us, that helps us to stand tall, to face our responsibilities and not live like the wounded child we have become. The shape shifting and creating anew will move us forward into a different age, a new body, a new appearance and we will begin to manifest our grown-up state.

Connecting to the body and finding movement in the dance is like a higher power itself, holding us as we enter into an ever-deepening journey. We are changed…

If we can learn to move with emotion, then we can begin to shift some of the stuck energy – energy-in-motion, e-motion, and breathe through trauma and tension. As we do this, memories might start to appear and we can write them down, recognising that they need some attention if they are to heal, not to get stuck with the one story, but to find a new way to shift its energy, possibly by finding new and different actions to take that remodel our way of thinking and create new neurological pathways in the brain.

We might take this dance out into the heart of nature, where we begin to find a different kind of teaching, a different kind of support. In the elements; earth, fire, water and air, we find the resources and the possibility of different sounds that are not the usual melodies of music, like deep belly sounds, the sounds of nature and the sound of our own breathing, voice and heart. We become more in touch with nature, in connection with ourselves and the very essence of life, as if we are returning to the life force that first bore us. And here we find more space and quietness, to enable us to listen and be still, to be more in touch with the ground we walk upon. Returning to nature helps us to tap into the ancientness of our own land, the history of our ancestors and the healing that needs to be done through our lineage that is appropriate to where we are on our journey.

There are always new landscapes to be found as they hold us in their embrace. The landscape becomes our teacher, both from our inner mind's eye and the portal of our imagination, to the outer territories of the hills, the mountains, the trees and the plant life. Included in all of this is the animal kingdom; the furred and the feathered, the four footed and the winged beings. The songs of the skies and the howls of the earth. And the richness of movement, for where there is movement there is life, life that must be respected and cherished. Its rich tapestry woven into every landscape, sharing the wisdom of an ancient connection to the visible face of spirit. And who do we become ourselves when we allow ourselves to connect so deeply to the living environment around us? What happens to the muscles and the bones of our own living organism, as we immerse ourselves into the fabric of nature? Only we can decide!

My own upbringing was close to nature, it is where I sought solace, connected to the dream time. And with the help of my animal friends, my pets and the spiritual guidance that was innate to me, I managed to adopt an attitude of respect for all living things. I felt others' pain, including the earth and animals and my ultra sensitive body would feel an honouring of these lives. But I also felt deeply overwhelmed by the pain and suffering, so much so that it created a shut-down in me, that became a habit and a pattern that was hard to clear at times.

As a child I always believed everything was real, everything had a soul. From my first teddies, to the tree in the Garden or a stone ornament, it all had meaning. It has been what taught me about Animism, which means all things and life forms possess a distinct spiritual essence. Potentially perceiving all things – animals, rocks, plants, rivers, weather systems, human handiwork and perhaps even words – as animated and alive. This I have never been able to or wished to let go of, yet often needing to adjust myself within this belief, as the ways of the world can create a shutting off from the pain they can inflict. The belief in Animism is deeply connected to indigenous ways, it is inherent in their belief systems. There is often no word to describe it, it just 'is'!

This sensitivity can be created by an animistic belief. So it will often create a need for solace and isolation, which nature can provide. But there can then remain an aloneness that does not always serve, partly due to the rejection of modern society because of such beliefs. This can be hard to let go of, as the one retreats into self and morosity.

I work to de-isolate myself, to be part of the world and its challenges, to open up to my part in it all and to play the role I am here to play.

Isolation can affect many of us.

Journeying into my own stories and being able to connect to the wounded part has given me insights into what I carry, which also enables me to humble myself, to drop the ego, to listen to my soul speaking through me and listen to the human and natural life around me. This enables me to embark on a journey to greater awareness, thus expanding my consciousness not just for my sake, but also for the good of my human and non-human connection.

We carry so much history and so many stories that it can be hard to humble ourselves to the experience of life, without demand and need for more.

Will all that we have, ever be enough?

To find the shapeshifter we must learn to listen and to meditate, to invite spirit in, to pay attention to what really matters and be the inspiration needed for others. Emptying out the old, or at least accepting what is old and finding its medicine – meaning that in the acceptance of it and the deeper acknowledgement and understanding of it, we recognise that the wounding of this experience serves a greater purpose. Thus we recognise it as part of the greater plan for our soul's offering, asking ourselves, 'What has it taught me? What has it shed light on in order for me to grow and in order for me to be able to share its medicine with other beings, or with the world?'

I take my work into places where simplicity and a hunger for healing through spontaneity, creativity and safety holds more value than the making and creating of plans, the setting of goals, and often the meaningless situations we can sometimes find ourselves in. I invite us all to step into the centre of our own light, to embrace the potential within us, to allow ourselves to shine.

How do we engage with our bodies and with our hearts when finding our dance? Not to be 'dancers' as in a performance way, but to free up our bodies and let the energy that has been deeply trapped inside of us begin to flow. Then we naturally become 'dancers' for ourselves – not to entertain or please others – but to feel the vitality from within, as well as the pain that moves as emotion through the body, releasing us from past trauma and climbing out from the deep crevices of shame.

To become like that shapeshifter we must learn how to empty the ego self and become our soul-full self, our God-centred self and allow source, universal energy, to become aligned within us. Then the ego can be useful and find its rightful actions. We learn that nothing is needed except for our willingness and our humility to life, the courage of our hearts and the commitment of the one who wishes to grow.

It doesn't mean all is done; we are not complete in any way for there is always new growth knocking at the door.

With all of this we give the ego a resting place, to only be useful for what really matters and focus on the meeting of ego and soul. Allowing our hands to become the essential carrier of our soul purpose, bringing our offering to the earth and giving us its rightful work to do, allowing our hands to lead us in the right direction.

The hands are connected to the heart, when our hands open and are free, so are our hearts. When our hands clench tightly, our hearts can clench too. They are a mirror of each other.

When soul and ego have fully met and are in line with each other there is a quickening. We find ourselves propelled in the very direction we have longed to go for many years.

We have been working towards this and putting in place what needs to happen, thus we find ourselves received and welcomed more fully in the place that 'fits' with the archetypal energies that we are. Who do we become then as the shape of us shifts into the being that lives more strongly now?

Fear can, of course, arise with the feeling of openness and a stronger connection to this and it can be somewhat unnerving. The energy can suddenly feel so huge that we are unsure how to hold it, yet we know that we must. It may meet with all manner of judgment and criticism from our fellow humans, yet still we keep going, watching out for that judgment, as it strikes a blow through our heart and gut.

Our solar plexus will feel the blows, yet our heart will endure because it has to. It knows it must and it pushes forward, creating each pathway one step at a time into unknown places, and places that have never before been trodden.

We step forward, preparing the way for our sovereignty, as the golden light of the innocent's crown lands more closely to our breast.

Sovereignty

My Sovereign hides a cloak of shame
Unsure of its royal place
Behind that veil
the wrongs have been done
those masks are worn to hide
To cover unacknowledged parts
the scorn of many faces
to feel my presence
in this place
no one can feel that pain
For all too long
my core won't shine
and dampen will my flame
I must undo what has been done
And seek the solace new

For midst the angst and faith to hold
a meaning is bestowed
What is my role – whats mine to show
I can no longer hide
But first the work from deep within
must wake my inner guide.

Are we not all desperately trying to reclaim our sovereignty?

Yet do we really know what it means? When I think of my own Sovereign, I think about myself as born with a soul in-tacked, of being complete and being loved for who I am, in God's eyes, never mind anyone else's!

And that love needed to continue, but did it continue and did I find a way to love myself and to accept myself fully?

Chances are we all began to lose some of the sovereignty of our birthright.

It is the way of the world and we end up, in so many different ways, trying to call back that inherent beautiful part of ourselves and fill ourselves up with self esteem, courage and love and all those things that help us to feel valued.

These days it seems to be money that makes us feel our value, or what we own, or how good our work is. I am so often in that place myself, when the work simply isn't there, the bank balance is low, no one is knocking at the door!

So without these things, how can we feel valuable just for who we are?

It doesn't always equate. And we need to live, right?

So what needs to change without pointing the finger and blaming others, or looking elsewhere for the answers? How can we look into ourselves and begin to find out what is really missing?

And then go to work on that part of ourselves to do what is necessary to rectify what is broken. We need to feel complete no matter what!

So within this work we begin to look at our personal myth, deepening the journey and allowing that archetypal myth to become the Sovereign of our birth right.

It is a lifetime's journey and we can be so fed up with trying to find the answers and it never quite meeting our needs, so we go from place to place, from workshop to training, to possessions or communities where we think we might find the answer, yet still, the same old stuff keeps rearing its head!

Maybe it's not what we are doing physically, but that old belief that keeps going round in our heads and what we attach to it. But it needs a different approach, maybe it needs a new way to behave with it, a new kind of discipline? Whatever it is, it is YOU that holds the key. Your myth, your dream, your life story.

That key has been carried by you for a lifetime, quite often in the rucksack on your back where it can't be seen, where it is hidden from view.

The adolescent-teenager, fighting to reclaim some dignity, some sense of purpose, some kind of esteem that will liberate and help to meet life with an honourable heart. It is hidden in the stories of the past, if we could just see a little more clearly into that innate wisdom we hold.

If we think of the golden crown of sovereignty, we see a golden reflection of completeness; a full circle, and this is the representation of ourselves as complete human beings. Nothing missing, a soul intact and open to life.

Your Sovereign is the key holder since birth and only you can open the door and let it back in. It's not necessarily easy, for there are paths to cross and mountains to climb, rivers and tides to swim against. Our main focus must be not to give up, to look for the many keyholes and listen for the call from the magic around us.

I know it is there for everyone and it is a beautiful journey to reclaim what is rightfully ours.

Becoming my own Sovereign with all of its responsibility would mark a very important time for me, a time to know I had arrived at the right place in my life and it was now time to take it on fully.

For it is the words and expressions of others that allow me to know if I am in my rightful place. I cannot fully decide that for myself.

This is the time for true healing. Can I let go? Can I deepen my connection to the mystery and surrender myself to the journey I have lived, leaving whatever is needed from it in the hands and dreams of those who follow?

To be sovereign I need to know myself and I need to know where my own offering comes from. What are its roots and foundations?

* * *

I now know much of what my purpose is. I know I am ready to live to the absolute potential of who I am, that I'm here for the music and dance of life, to be the writer I have longed to be since childhood. And it is quite simple, something that doesn't need a bandstand. It doesn't need naming in gold and it's just simply what makes me happy.

That is how we know what we are here for – whatever makes us truly joyful.

I believe in dance, poetry and music as a life force, the very things that create joy and happiness within us. We need music and creativity to awaken us, to bring us to life, to show us what really matters!

And life to me is as close as it gets to spiritual practice. I'm not much of an advocate for 'doing a daily practice'. For me it would be far too easy to do my practice and then forget about it for the rest of the day! So I tend to aspire to 'live' my practice. To live it on a daily basis, bringing my beliefs into daily living and being as honourable and as principled as I can possibly be, to the life I am living and have been blessed with.

And I make mistakes as well and plenty of them. Still, I believe the best way forward is to simply do our best, from moment to moment.

So what is my offering?

To do what is mine and only mine to do in the world. My story has shown me the path, alongside the need to create that most important offering.

It is my creativity and passion that will change the world for the better!

Can we believe this? Can we take it in, embody it and learn to walk its talk?

* * *

Creativity, dance and movement, body connection and an open heart is at the core of this work. We engage with the free dancing and creative spirit, whatever ability or age we are. There is a feeling that goes with this that awakens the potential within us. We witness our own dance as well as the dance of others, we observe the creative in all walks of life. We become mirrors for each other and we allow the information discovered to inform our soul's journey.

We can meditate on what we have witnessed. This nourishes us and we discover more of its power, along with the words from our hearts and our experiences, all that we have gathered to us and all that it has taught us about ourselves.

The art of acceptance gets easier with this way of being in the world, to see, to listen and to be at peace with whatever the outcomes.

We are learning.

Learning acceptance to live a natural way and to know that all is well, even in the most difficult of moments. That Spirit/ God is with us. It helps us to take away blame or criticism of others. Our judgements soften, we receive each other without feeling threatened or competitive. This is the root of spirituality, if we can see each other as God's children.

I have a loving relationship with God, as I understand God to be. I accept that I am the one that God intended me to be, there can be no comparison made with anyone else.

The belief in a higher power, a force greater than myself keeps me humble, and prevents me getting caught in my own ego and any thought that I might be able to 'play God' in my life or anyone else's. God has been with me since childhood. I prayed as a child, was fascinated with nuns and I wanted something that they had; a connection, a life source, the deepest prayer. Whatever it was, I wanted it.

And so from this place I make my offering, which is the path of Middle Earth Medicine and the Magic Of Mandorla, taking others on a journey, teaching a way to live our lives creatively, with less stress, anxiety and pressure to be a certain way. To adopt 'mindfulness' in all that we do, think and feel. It is a practice that we live – not do on occasions or at a certain time each day. It is learning to be a Seer, the Seer that is at the centre of the Mandorla, in the centre of the Wheel, a witness to the whole picture of our lives. To give attention to our past stories and what we need to accept, and then to focus on what needs to change.

The work of the Wheel follows a guideline of ethics and principles, that weave together an authentic way of living, exercising mindfulness, observing our interactions with others, our connections to what is around us and how we behave. This path is about learning to be a fulfilled human and what it actually takes to accomplish that. It means living a spiritual life as well as a life of mundanity; a marriage of soul and ego. These two need to dwell together and become the well centred ego and the embodied soul, the healthy aspects of each. Ego without soul is focused on material gain, or only interested in self. Soul with no ego can become lost, drifting into a world of pure fantasy. A life that involves service is needed, where the ego becomes the hands of the soul. It means a very deep connection to the heart, to the mind and to the body, and if we are truly to grow, then we learn to take full responsibility for our actions.

And taking responsibility means that we need to address behaviours that do not serve us or others. Not just knowing it but acting on it, otherwise we leave a superficial understanding of it without finding out how to change it. Knowing it is one thing, but doing the work necessary on it is another.

If we live with negative or bad thoughts about others, if we are using resources beyond our true needs, if we take part in actions that are harmful for humanity, for animals, for nature, lacking mindfulness in what we do – might we need to adopt the willingness to change?

Do we have the courage to grow, to develop our purpose and reason for being here by making those changes?

This is also taking responsibility so we are not totally dependent on others, to grow into all we can be through our own efforts, hard work and perseverance – to be the best human being possible. What kind of life do we receive if we don't? Are we even grateful for the life we have been given?

Our journey might mean less 'playing safe', which means shining our own light, without hiding behind a mask of 'niceness', and exploring our own sovereignty. To live our soul's calling, marrying our core wounds with our own aspirations and allowing our soul and our ego to live in harmony. It also means setting harms to right and changing our bad habits. And can we do all of this, yet remain conscious and aware of the welfare of those around us, as well as our environment, for then our sovereignty cannot be harmful to others.

This is not always such an easy task and requires presence, the total presence of standing in the centre of our own circle.

The Mandorla, known as the almond shape of light that surrounds a holy or spiritual figure, is the symbol of pure presence. In this work we often talk about our circle of support and resources, an energy field where we gather to us our own particular needs, an energetic sphere, that is protective as well as illuminating; it helps us to find insights into what is it we need on a personal level. And this Mandorla process of bringing the two together, I realised, was the symbol representing the polarities that I had been experiencing throughout my life. This art of being with this symbol of energy is the ability to be with all that is, the positive and the negative, to be with the tension of opposites.

Surrendering to that tension creates pain and pleasure, which is the true experience of ecstasy, the great orgasm of life which many would try to escape from. The discomfort being far too much to bear. But bear it we must if we really wish to live, if we really wish to be free!

It is known as one of the most powerful of (spiritual) experiences we can have in life. The Mandorla is the place of poetry 'where the fire and the rose are one!' (Four Quartets, T.S. Eliot).

The rose represents royalty or sovereignty, and divine love. The fire is the divine harshness and the spiritual ether, which is capable of purifying the human soul. They come together in all their divinity, the Sovereign becoming purified within that light, which offers us freedom and the absence of limitations, if for a moment.

'And all shall be well and all manner of things shall be well when the tongues of flame are in-folded into the crowned knot of fire and the fire and the rose are one.' (Four Quartets, T.S. Eliot)

And so we put one foot in front of the other, we accept the holy mantle of the healing path and we begin to embark on a journey to meet with the tension. We become the edgewalkers, walking between worlds with the ability to build bridges across and between those differences and circles of life. Those with a strong inner life who know themselves well, grounded and effective in their world. Those shapeshifters that seek the re-connection with their own Sovereign, their own sacred rose.

As we come to this realisation, the journey shows itself as a path that may well rock our shores and we might wonder why we wouldn't choose a more simplistic easy life, one of mundanity and ordinariness. But if it has called to us, though we resist for a while, we will ultimately surrender to it eventually, knowing it is not possible to walk away, to go back to sleep, for the tug at the heart is too great. We know we must take a look outside the box, we must push our edges of discomfort, allowing this tension to scourge our muscles and bones, letting the heart ache in its turmoil. Then we know we are growing, we are becoming our true nature.

* * *

Even those who are highly successful can lose their connection to their spirituality, thus making something 'other' become their God, which can often be wealth and glamour as well as their own social status. Losing sight of their ultimate purpose means that the soul's contract first birthed, which this book addresses, becomes lost, fragmented or forgotten.

Notes

Sovereign Leadership

In my experience of many different trainings and learning about different modalities, I have learnt to question everything, but it took me a while to do so.

There is a spiritual quality in what I do because I am connected to God, not out of a sense of being spiritually guru-like or having gurus, or that I am higher than anyone else, but because I am broken! Yes, literally, I am broken to the core. I am nothing and I am everything, I am small and humble and I am extraordinarily larger than life. I do my best to put myself out there on the stage of life and I need to remember that I am one of the herd.

I am not separate.

My brokenness allows me to see the story of where I have come from, what lies in my wounded innocence. It allows me to have spiritual awakenings and discover the innate wisdom within. And as someone who watches over the needs of others in my workshops and offerings, I need to be even more so aware of this. If my offering to the world ever became more than my vocation, my soul's calling, then I might need to keep it in check.

* * *

In most organisations, I am left wondering and questioning; what is hierarchical and what is egalitarian? These days I have found the need to question the leaders and teachers, in every interaction.

Years ago I found myself thinking that they were always right, because they had charisma, because they seemed to be the ones that know, because they had authority.

Did I like authority?

And then I realised I was simply not in my own strength, I was not in my power. At times I was giving myself away. I was not adopting my own strength and ability. I wasn't taking responsibility for myself. I was hooked into someone else's charisma and I was aspiring towards them, not to the embodied sense of my own true nature and innate wisdom. My adoration of the one that I had put on that pedestal was causing me pain and taking me away from my own serenity.

Oh dear authority,
you break our spirit
and un-free our soul,
you hold our hand like a doting mother
who only wants for her own satisfaction,
her pleasure
and her need to be right!

We need leaders, it is vital in our communities. We need people who can lead without diminishing others, those who can step down and out of the way, allowing others with more experience to step forward. Giving away that leadership position when it is right and correct to do so.

Good leadership is about being dedicated, with the ability to take effective action in many different circumstances. And if the leader is unable to do this, then it is time to step aside and let another step forward.

We might support a leader who is disciplined in this manner, but rarely find it easy to support the one who is power-driven and has no judgement or understanding of his actions or his dysfunctions. He may never be satisfied, unless he has power over all.

He/she may remain in this position for a long while, but not gain the full respect that is required. If he or she does not own that blinkered view freely, naming those flaws and defects, owning up to mistakes and wrongs, then those who find themselves able to peel away from the grip of that holding force, will do so without a second glance.

There are leaders who demand, seduce, manipulate others. They may do this very cleverly and creatively, making the student, the worker or whoever he/she is, feel somehow indebted. The student will be overly willing to serve and will do anything asked for. This is much like the child of a narcissistic parent, who isseen as an extension of them, and therefore must perform and meet unrealistic expectations!

Then there is cultish behaviour of leaders who give that small nugget of love, bestowing generously when it suits them and then withholding that love and generosity, leaving the 'less loved child' that often ends up at this table, in the grip of needing and wanting more, hungrily chasing the dream that is never fulfilled.

This is not leadership at all even though it can be very confusing and convincing when in its grip!

I've been there. I've witnessed this kind of so-called skill and it is not pretty! Yet it is very easy to fall for, particularly when rewards are offered and promises are made for the future.

I've had to learn from these dysfunctions in our society and have fallen a few times for those organisations' 'skills', and it is from this that I am doing my best to create something around leadership that is very different.

I created a map that was connected to my own life story. I trusted that this was spirit led and now it is my job to pass it on to others. I believe that it is only by being able to offer it to others, that I can really find true leadership qualities. It does not mean I must starve for my cause, but how much that wage is, is another matter. For if our leaders are so well financed in their life, and their workers are not, then there is no balance and someone is being robbed. This will soon hint of a cult-guru system that gives its leaders a very prosperous way of life, while others struggle, unable to find their way out of a deep pit of monetary debt.

Still more will be asked of them, insisting that in the end they would become as well positioned as the leaders themselves. Many promises will be made. Spiritual sickness ensues and the gurus get rich and those who are brave enough to step away will do so. And those who fall into the play of those elite power-hungry games, give their souls away like martyrs to what they think is a very good cause.

And woe betide the one who grows, for they will be frowned upon.

Notes

New Leaders and Sovereignty

If we are to embrace our sovereignty, then we need to go way, way back to that 'Crown in the Magical Garden'.

The Crown represents our innocence, the re-birth of our purity, landing here in the Magical Garden that is our earth. We begin to remember our first loves and what helped us to find them. Mine was poetry, the dance and how I struggled to write with the perfection of my mother, whilst holding on for dear life to my own voice. It took a long time before I could fully allow it to flow, to trust it would be received and claim myself as the writer I knew I had dreamt into being. I need a voice in the world, and this was the way I could have that voice.

This was me at my most sovereign and it would take a lot to fully reclaim that through my own quest. And what would I do with it? In time I began to hold the space for others to bring out their creative purpose, to show their crown to the world and support them to fully shine with their purpose.

That filled me with joy, to witness those passions being reignited that had once been shut down and forced to shut-up, for whatever reason.

Leadership comes from knowing ourselves at the level of sovereignty, because we cannot lead without knowing ourselves. And we need to know that mythological story, so we can find the archetype and the purpose and learn to embody it.

* * *

As I sit beside the seashore on a stony beach, I reach in and feel the stones around me, some of them so worn by the ocean's waves and currents, that there is an incredible softness. No hard edges or corners, just pebbled into smoothness.

My hands feel seduced by this and it softens me, and my heart.

Yet in the softening I know that the mightiest of powers have created it this way.

Looking out across the waves towards the horizon, I am awed by this great mass of water stretching beyond what the eye can see. And without the other elements it would not have the life that it has.

Isn't this what power really looks and feels like, the ability to weave and blend with all it is connected to and the ability to soften even the hardest rock and the tightest of hearts?

The stillness is needed to be able to listen and observe – to simply be quiet.

And then the force of the waves rising above
the tides, the crashing waters,
where no sound ever went before
It's pioneering, potentially destructive
cleansing of the plastic and poison it meets
along the way,
embarking on sodden shores
we witness and we listen…
the power to observe arrives

The power subsides,
It is known
exactly
what to do

In our own culture we witness what has been thought to be 'power', where our leaders have not earned our respect easily, if at all, in these last decades.

Leaders are so often led only by ego, by the need to be seen, to be heard and to be acknowledged. If we are to come from the soul, then there is no need for this, because we know we are seen, heard and acknowledged by God.

There is nothing more needed, we do not need to meet with others' approval, but we do need their agreement for us to stand in leadership. They will follow with joy, not because it is forced upon them but because they aspire to be as that leader is and it encourages them.

And a true leader will know when the time is right to step back and allow others to step forward, to be seen, heard and acknowledged for who they are as leaders.

Many find this hard simply because it is a threat to their status.

As leaders we will make mistakes, like any other human, but the healthy leader will know how to deal with that mistake, making it as right as can be and taking council with those who have gone before.

So often we ridicule our leaders, disrespecting and disbelieving them. It has become the sign of our times that a new leadership is needed on this threshold. If we are to look around ourselves and ask what that powerful position might need, we have only to learn from the natural forces around us.

It has been considered that in order to stand in a leadership role, whether through politics or ministerial roles, or corporations and organisations, then monetary wealth must be at the forefront.

Yet, if we look at what is truly powerful around us, there is very little materialistic wealth or finance behind it.

If we look at what truly touches our hearts, without alluring and seducing us into its web, we would see something very different to what we assume is power.

And it is becoming very clear that many of today's leaders are running with broken stories of the past, not turning towards the healing of those life stories and unpacking some of the dysfunction, trauma and neglect that has taken place. The story then runs in the planning of business and leadership within countries, where often we laugh at their antics. Possibly laughing at what we see of ourselves and our own dysfunctions, who knows for sure. But one thing that is quite clear, is that unless the stories find the healing needed, then the circulating stories of denial will keep rotating, and the same wounds will be inflicted over and over again, causing dysfunction within our workplace and our countries.

Coming back to my story at the seaside, where I planted that small stone amidst the other stones, I invited the seed of my words to metaphorically find root, and for the power of those words to bring forth a little more magic.

I sit there with my small ritual, aware of the relationship between the stone and the mighty ocean, the many millions of stones on this one beach connected to thousands of other beaches and landscapes around the world. I am aware of a world of softly smoothed stones, the ocean that has sculpted them. The ebbing and flowing of tides and the great force of something that humans cannot endure, those depths that can take lives, that no man has any power over.

I am aware of the fishermen who live alongside these waves, the weathered brows and tousled hair, the sun battered skin and the salty taste of treacherous journeys. They have met with much and life has shown them the darkness and the fruitfulness of those depths. How much do they know from life, just like the miners, the mountain climbers, the explorers, those who ride the ocean waves and those who have worked passionately and then lost it all?

What can they share with us of leadership, of comradeship and of truly meeting life's grit?

Those who have come to the edge and know the true meaning of life!

Where will humour lie with this one? Where will they get to see themselves so much more clearly? Where will their life rush before them, revealing old stories and memories in sudden moments of near death? When will they pray so much more deeply in moments of terror? When will they long to be home by the fireside, wondering if they will see their family again?

Can those who have met with this grit of life, stand up and tell us their story? And can those who believe that they understand life so much better, sit in waiting, trying a little harder with what it means to lead from a broken heart, a knowing heart, a heart that has bled for its worth?

There is a shadow of spiritual leadership that hides away, unseen and we must be careful of this, both in ourselves and in how we are led by others.

Giving ourselves away, surrendering our own power are both makings of this shadow. But so too is making others our Gods.

If we put somebody in between us and our true God or Higher Spirit, if we put them on that pedestal too high, then we will never really find what is ours to do.

It can be hard to recognise this. So how do we support this to happen? Someone appears to have what we want and so we want to know how to find it for ourselves. It is natural to go to learn from them, but then that can become dysfunctional, because our growth might threaten theirs. We may become too dependent, unable to move on, with no idea why we cannot do so. We linger, caught in a trap of our own making, not able to release ourselves, or take out the hooks and our true nature; the reason we are really there, becomes lost.

Caretaker or Space Holder

How many of us had displacement of responsibility as children? How many of us were reversed in our care-taking? Our parents were there to take care of us, yet some part of us believed that it was up to us to take care of our parents. And in some cases, where a parent was unwell or disabled, then it figured that this would be necessary. But what I am talking about is the care-taking that was hidden, inverted, introverted enabling and certainly not spoken about or supported.

As I grew up I knew full well that I was being sexually abused, but I could not tell anyone until much later in life. I felt I needed to protect my father from knowing about what his father was doing to his daughter, as I felt he would not be able to cope with it.

I had witnessed his father – my grandfather – belittling him, talking down to him, being unkind to him and I did not want to add to this.

Maybe in hindsight, had I told my father, he may have had the choice to stand up to his father. To be the protective father he needed to be and clearly the protective father that I needed him to be as well.

Maybe I would have been of greater service to my father had I done that, giving him the opportunity to step up and not be so defeated as a son. But that is not mine to try to change or control, it is not mine to try to fix my father.

So this became my own healing to deal with, to look at how in later years I protected men from discomfort. This was not mine to do either, but was left over from this pattern I held from childhood.

I could now only learn from this experience and try to ensure it did not continue with my adult relationships.

If we look at our own need to care-take, we might find in the woven threads of our life story the reason why we chose to lead, to hold space, to share what we know, to be a space holder or a leader or even a care-giver.

This can lie in the shadows of our offering if we are not careful.

The young child in us might still be trying to work it out.

So then we start to look at where we try to heal, to take over, to control and believe that we have the answers for others' lives. It can become manipulation if we are not careful.

Exploring the dark realms of our past is very necessary. Turning over the rocks and looking into the crannies of our stories, we uncover the hidden experiences that remind us of who we are and why we are really here.

As long as we know those stories, they cannot control us or lurk in the background, where they become dysfunctions and where our mistakes are often made.

Becoming a space holder or leader for others means a lot of responsibility rests in our hands. It is no small thing. Yet for the majority of professions of people taking care of others, there are no prerequisites for people to have to do their inner work, to get to know their own story and to heal a difficult or traumatic life. It simply has not been made an important part of our culture's leadership roles or part of how we seek and find our work or our vocation.

What is appropriate for us as individuals to offer to others?

Most of us hold projections, ill-feelings or resentments towards other people. This will filter into what we are offering and will affect the work we do with the people involved.

We might ask, who is standing behind the person I am feeling distaste towards? Who is it from the past that reminds me of this person or these actions? Is it even myself? And I may need to take stock, to be honest, to detach from what is in front of me and address what is my own work to do.

So I look to the past and uncover the times that I have acted in a way that is similar to what I see before me.

When was I unkind, or arrogant, selfish or grandiose? When did I get angry or when did I laugh at someone unkindly without love?

There is a way to stand in the centre of two circles, where one circle can represent a gateway energy; an emotion or difficult sensation. Then there is a circle that represents where we would like to get to.

I might feel a lot of anger, so I might wish to arrive at a place of peacefulness with a person, group or even object.

I do not want to dismiss the anger entirely because this would not be healthy. So I stand within the anger circle to feel all that this emotion is showing me about myself. I find creative expression from it. I find its voice and I give it permission.

In the other circle I hold the place I wish to arrive at, the place of peace with the anger. I step into that circle and I might ask, what is needed to bring me to this place?

I find its creative expression.

I go between these two circles, exploring their creative outlets. I honour each one and give them permission to be just as they are.

I then bring myself into the centre where these two circles overlap, what do I find here as they both merge with each other? What does this show me about myself?

I might move with this energy, in the light of where the two circles meet, finding a creative form to write with, to make art with, to sing with or simply to dance with.

What do I discover?

Most importantly, I take responsibility for all of my emotions, for all of my stories. And I take the blame and projections away from others until I am totally clear about what I am responsible for. And as long as I do my work, then I am in a healthy place to be able to lead others, to hold a safe space for others, to ensure that my 'inflated' ego is not getting in the way.

So to become sovereign means taking complete responsibility for myself and my life as a mature adult. It is up to me to do the work that is mine to do.

As a good leader we must know that great ideas and brilliant plans can come from anyone and anywhere. It is up to the leader to encourage others to step forward. If the leader is only power driven and lining his or her own pocket with the wealth of the organisation, then it is not leadership at all but mendacity.

As a healthy leader, one may need to let go of some of the ideas that have been held close and step aside, as others find what is theirs to do.

Notes

The Sacredness of the Fool

And when that leader arrives at their sovereignty, let us hope that there will be a connection to their Sacred Fool, the one who can chuckle at themselves in private moments even when the heart feels ashamed, or who can share a story about their follies, owning up to where they went wrong and finding a little humour in that – at no one else's expense. Their Sacred Fool helps them to digest their life's journey with a greater understanding and wisdom. The 'elephant in the room' must be recognised and only the Sacred Fool can truly magnify this, in a way that helps the heart to stay open and see clearly.

Our healthy Sacred Fool is wise without a doubt, telling the truth in a way that can be spoken with humour. There is no need for the Fool to worry about what others think, as the truth must be unveiled.

We might act the part of foolishness, merely to evoke a truth telling that is kinder and more bearable to the one who hears. And we will most certainly be very well equipped to laugh at our own humanness, at our own playing at life.

My ego will indeed have met with the Sacred Fool, as it strips me of my need to be right, my need for gain, my need for power. The Sacred Fool will help me to unveil what is hidden, for it allows nothing to pass me by. For is not power simply a way to be above others, to control, to be right, to play God in my own community, to be enslaved to a world where there is no going back?

Being that Shapeshifter I must change my shape and adopt the humorous and free-speaking voice. I must know myself on every level and I must be willing to face up to my mistakes no matter how humiliating that is.

I am human, I am not infallible, I screw up and have dysfunctional behaviours that travel with me across the years. If I become aware of them in whatever form they take, then I must own up to them. And over time, as I adopt a new action to take their place, I settle.

And within that settling I will be reminded of where I come from, not just my family of origin but even my prehistoric society, my tribal connections and the law of the land I reside in. From here I will grow towards the elder I need to be, not serious and outspoken, but with a jolly heart and a deeper understanding of those around me who need my stories to help remind them of their own.

Our Fool will turn our heads to the tragedy of life, to the masks we have chosen to wear. And in gentle moments, as the truth seeps into the corners of a smile, the failure will seek a different kind of witness and tears of joy might prevail. Our deeply human, silly, uncontrolled ways of behaving will take stock as the light is shone and all is revealed. From this moment, with humour as our resource, we are seen and we cannot step back. What is lost is lost, we turn a page and at that moment the weight falls, the teardrops and the smile, newly discovered, we leap through the gateway of a new beginning. And this feeling of relief strikes a chord in our hearts, as we recognise that we now know ourselves a little better.

All of those failures, all of those losses are known, and the arrogance that we thought we could hide them away, diminishes.

We must resource ourselves well with that humor, for it will be so necessary as the crystal becomes clearer and we can see through it all.

Our Sovereign will need this one, connected closely by its side, for this one has no seeking of power, it seeks to simply honour what is true.

No need for false compliments, the Sovereign needs the truth in order to be of better service.

Those valuable insights will shatter the illusions that prevailed and jest becomes a little more attractive as it knows the power of truth and revels in its glory.

It is a bitter taste we hold in our mouths, a bitter taste that is held for only a moment, until it spits itself away from those lips. With a knowing look and a sigh of contempt for who we were, that must not last too long, for we know it was sometimes necessary to act in those ways. It is how we learnt to survive, and survive we had to, if our soul was to live and inhabit this body.

Laughter will soften and aid the healing of what was old with perfect timing. We cannot laugh alone, for a witness's eye must help us over that threshold. As it is in the being witnessed that the excruciating pain can also be felt.

Ah, we have been seen, we cannot hide. No, we absolutely cannot hide our shadow self, for it has been revealed and lies in the shadows no more, it has been set free, our destructive-self is no more.

* * *

It would take me quite some time to heal some of the agonies I felt, having made mistakes, having upset the apple cart of my life. The only way to truly heal, was to fully digest my own story, to the point where I really could eventually laugh at myself. I could tell the story without it hurting, without feeling shame, without any need to tell the story in any other way.

So I could turn it around and create an offering to others from it. This is where I was, this is what I have done about it and this is how I feel about it now. And to be able to smile about it because it no longer controls me, it no longer resides in the back seat of my life, driving this vehicle forwards, causing havoc in its midst.

We feel the pain and embarrassment, the discord that pulls at our heart. We shrink from being seen and we need to hide, yet in fact, in between the pain, the tears and the feelings of failure, a moment of liberation is felt. It has to be that right moment, when something changes, there is laughter, we cannot help it, and a smile appears and we know! We step through the opening door of our heart and into the light as freedom takes our hand.

One step and we are free.

Many steps and we can change our lives.

The Aspiring Elder

The Wise Elder will nod at these recompenses and help steer our Sovereign to make better these failings of the human condition, leaning that one into being of better service to his or her people. Encouraging that one to serve the Innocent and to enter into the mystery that supports the Dreamer. Standing, staff in hand the Elder is able to tell stories of a lifetime, reaching well into the heart and soul of the Sovereign, inspiring this one to awaken fully, to dream a bigger dream and to wish for that better future for all.

With no wish for oneself, the Wise Elder is in total service, simple to the core with dreams of yesteryear and a willingness to surrender to that greatest teacher of all, Death.

Growing ourselves into eldership with an integrated and digested life story, I consider to be one of the most important aspects of our work.

Some of our cultures, it seems, are missing out on what can be gained from eldership. Partly because we no longer respect elders as we once did, and because there is a huge separation between families. Grandparents can live far away from the homes of grandchildren, the miles between us having grown due to us being able to travel more, to live where our work is, or wherever we choose to be. There is much more freedom these days.

And it is not just the family who move away, some grandparents move because of work and of course many other reasons. My own grandparents moved away to the sea because of health, they were lucky that we were able to visit regularly, but that would not be so for many families.

It might also be because family systems have broken down. So much dysfunction and little support leaves families in conflict and separation. Addictions, different belief systems in different generations, divorces, the need to control, infidelity, workaholism, all manner of sickness can and will leave families estranged.

So how do we learn to look forward to eldership in today's society? How might we find a way through some of the difficulties and continue with our lives, growing into eldership, as it would be intended for us.

Grandparenting is one of the most beautiful, exquisite experiences that I know, and like anything else, not without its need for awareness, strength, prayers and hopes.

I have a deep and loving connection with my grandchildren, as many grandparents do, that is different to anything else I feel. A love for them that connects strongly to my pulsing heart, like a deep concern and the protectiveness of an old aging lioness. I feel joy at everything they do and I laugh at funny, even naughty antics that as a parent I might not have been so accepting of. I can tolerate a lot more these days. I'm more patient and am more able to give a different kind of undivided attention that I could not have done so easily before, what with the washing to be done and cleaning the house, taxi servicing and multiple layered mothering roles.

Now there is time to focus simply on the one who wants some granny attention.

I do not see each one of my grandchildren as regularly as I would like, yet still they are a big part of my life.

I have moments to remind me of how my heart connects to being a grandmother, remembering the phone call from my son, the one that says 'baby is here'. It's a soft gentle voice no matter how big the son is, his voice is gentler and softer, as if he has been to the most magical of places and I can feel his smile spread down the phone-line and into my heart, we have a moment together as tears come to my eyes. 'Congratulations', I say equaling his softness as if no one else should hear. I'm so happy to hear the news and I am swift to pack a bag and head in that direction, if I can, to give any support if needed or just to look into those little eyes and make our acquaintance. Holding a newborn grandchild is something special indeed. My heart will leap a little and curl its tendrons around this little soul, with a deeply nurturing and loving acceptance of all that he or she is. Knowing this is the fruit of my own child, and has come through these lineages to join us all together, it is indeed a blessing.

I am blessed that my sons and daughters with a child, now know a little bit more about me and what it has meant to me to birth and bring them into the world. They know the unconditional love that they have for their family is what I have lived with for most of my life. This unconditional love is now there in my heart for my grandchildren. Of course I can hand them over and get on with the other parts of my life, but the love doesn't leave, and the thoughts and the preciousness of this life do not go away.

'Did you ever believe you could love this deeply?', I once asked my daughter.

Sharing a birthing experience with my daughter as she brings her little one to the world I am in awe of my own child's strength, but she is a mature woman now and I can no longer see her as a child.

We have been through the same experience. We know each other a little better. My grandson, born as I held his mother in my arms, even remembering his tiny bottom cradled in my hand as I supported their first meeting, witnessing the sense of awe in his eyes as he stared at his beautiful mother, was an unforgettable moment.

Exhausted from a long night and two days of hanging in there for them both, I'm relieved when rest finally comes, but still I want to be back there ensuring that all is well as if there is a compulsion somehow, to watch over... just incase I am needed. And I know to back off and allow young mum to find her way, even through the difficulties; because that is, as mothers know, what makes us stronger.

And holding back as they find their way, I am rewarded with the look in her eyes or my son's as they bond with their little one. It opens my heart immensely. How much prouder can I possibly be? Such a touching experience to witness.

And I don't always get it right, for that stepping back is often hard to do. I am conditioned to be that busybody mother-hen, who wants to support, take care of and rescue, which is the very thing I cannot allow myself to do. For every one of my friends and family must find their own way in life. I cannot make any assumption that I know what is right for another!

And this is my learning to do, no matter how big my addiction is to sorting out other people's problems, I remind myself and ask… 'What is truly mine to do here?'

There is the grandchild that lives far away and I am eternally grateful for the internet allowing me to know something of her and share messages from afar. Maybe one day we will meet in the flesh and I pray for that. Until then it is a journey of loving from afar, and only when circumstances allow can I know who we are together. I do my best, as only I can, always remembering that no matter what, we are connected and it will always be that way. We are connected through DNA and a link to our ancestors, our connection will remain in the lineage of our timelines and the history between the families of old.

What might my ancestors today think of this situation? What would SHE think of my grandparenting? The extended families of those days would more than likely share those same kitchens and backyards, maybe work the same fields and share in the abundance of their crops. The grandparents would watch their families grow and be so much more hands on when needed, as mothers washed clothing, as grannies cooked and mended, as fathers and grandfathers worked alongside each other in the factories and came home together to be greeted with those smiles. Well maybe not always, but I recognise my own fantasy of that extended family unit and the possibility of being more hands on a daily or weekly basis in my grandchildren's lives. I am a different being. I travel as I work, and in this day and age of workshops and gatherings, of living far apart from each other simply because we can, roaming countries more easily – it makes for a different way to stay connected to our families.

And then there is the grandchild I may never see again, because of a different circumstance, but one letter a year tells me all is well and an adoptive loving family ensures this, until the day she makes a decision for herself. I met her and held her once, a cuddle, a kiss, a little play with toy bricks. We got on well and with a heart wrenching goodbye, I cried. My love is still tied to that little soul who shares my blood but not my life. Maybe one day, who knows, she will know that I have thought about her every day and that there is a little light inside of me just for her. She will know her blood family if she wishes to, that I can most definitely ensure.

The teenager grandchildren – we have our own relationship now. They gently find their way to adulthood and we can communicate in a new way. I am here for them and it is now they who decide when to see me, when to acknowledge me, when it works best for them. My door is always open to them, and I love the feeling of witnessing their growth, of becoming the young people that they need to be. My eldest, a grandson, is a charming sweet young man. He tells me he loves me and I believe him. We both know something of youth and I've watched his parents grow together becoming young parents themselves. I'm fascinated with how he meets life and all that he is becoming.

From the very first moment a grandchild is born, I am observing who this little one is, who this child is becoming, what their own gifts might be and what is theirs to offer. That is a privilege!

I am also aware of how important it is for my sons and daughters to have the last say with their children's upbringing and not to interfere or make demands from my own opinions. My opinions must be kept to myself, unless I am asked for my experience, or my thoughts to share. If I notice an opinion bursting through, I must rein it in, put it elsewhere and leave it well alone – for the diminishing of the parents' own authority is unhealthy for everyone and will not serve the family dynamic.

And that can be hard, but not impossible, if not heeded it will only cause grief and upset, it will only alienate the parents and grandparents and cause problems with the bonding of babies to family.

My own life experience with this has taught me much. When my first born arrived it was a difficult time, particularly as a sixteen year old. I was very young, not prepared to be a parent at all, but it happened and I took it on as bravely as I could. I had a blind boyfriend and much to look after. His family took over the care of this little one. He was taken from my arms as I managed my boyfriend's needs. It was many years later that I had the realisation that what happened was not right, roles were reversed and mixed up. How much better it would have been if they had supported their own family member, their son and brother and allowed and encouraged me to look after my own baby, to be the young mum I needed to be.

My confidence was shattered. I felt they knew best. I was watched with every move, until I could only do what I could; to lead a blind man, to care for his needs, forever giving too much to this circumstance that was unhealthy for all. I didn't look after my baby, except at night when all others were asleep and it was there that I sang and cooed to him, the time I could cuddle him without making another jealous. The time I had to be with him all by myself.

Young mums need to find their own way, to be able to ask for support when they need it and not to have this first experience taken away from them, as it was for me.

There is so much to learn for all of us, as we encourage those around us, no matter how much we love them, or how much we feel we should support, we must let go of the control, to learn to let be, even when things look not quite as we would have them. Remembering that we are not the parents and not necessarily the best judge of what is happening, no matter how much experience we have. Unless of course there is real danger, it is not our job. Our job is to be the grandparent, to be all loving, supporting and trusting of our sons and daughters with their own decisions and ways of doing things.

And another important aspect of granny-hood is that I must know and connect to my own life, my own hobbies and interests, my work, my life with my husband and my own friendships. To not be dependent on my children or my grandchildren to meet my aging needs. I have a career, my own home and relationship, I have my writing and my offering to keep ahead of. I know I must look after my own purpose that incorporates being a granny, whilst knowing that it is not all that I am.

I have attended births and deaths and held many ceremonial gatherings. I have played with children both young and old. I have walked the path of nourishing the soul and assisted the many gateways and transitions that life offers us. And there is always more for me to learn.

Transitions between experience and the bridging of what that means is essentially my medicine, my offering and my own passion.

Walking on the edge between the worlds of birth and death is the journey of my own soul's purpose and as a mother to six and a grandmother to eight at this time, maybe more as time goes by, I am doing what feels most important. To be a good granny, to be connected to God and to love my family beyond measure, wherever they are in the world.

This is one aspect of aging and aspiring to eldership, but not the only part. For many of us will not be grandparents, or even have those families to rear. Some by choice and some not by choice.

But for all of us, we will age, if we are lucky enough. Our bodies will change and we will go from that youthful abundance to the slowing down, the tiredness and the bones of deep maturity.

How will that be for us? We can only at times imagine, as we witness those around us whose lives have moved on.

And of course everyone is different and every story is different. But one thing I am most curious about is whether we will reach our Elderhood content and happy with having digested our soul's purpose and living to the fullness of our journey here on earth. Will we have done the things we felt were important to do?

We might ask many of these questions also: will I be attractive and will I retain my looks? Will I be loved, even wanted? How will my body fare with changing skin and flesh, the muscular loss and the greying of hair? And also relating to eldership, the loss of career, which might be a very welcome retirement, or it might feel like a deep loss. Everyone will have his or her own story about this.

I love to witness our elders and I take pleasure from some with their simplicity of life. And I look to myself for signs of aging and learning to understand this time of surrender and acceptance for who we are.

Of course looks have a measure and we are brought up in this part of the world to idealise the young and youthful, being drawn away from the reality of life.

But that is not what truly makes my heart sing. No, it is the soul and spirit that I am truly drawn to and if I live in a world of comparison then I am doomed to a life that is in conflict. If I desire in any shape or form to be as others are, with younger bodies, skin and muscular tone, then I am raging with an enemy that I have absolutely no power over. My body will age, I will grow older and I must learn to love and accept that and humble myself to one of the greatest teachers in life. The great surrender, letting go of the human obsession around the body.

In our culture we are obsessed by how the body looks and how to avoid ageing.

We can try to battle the ageing process, but a battle it will be and we will not grow old gracefully. The battle may appear on the outside as a job well done, but inside there will be torment and knowing that it is not the truth.

We can always hide the truth, but it will get to us in the end!

Once we can accept ourselves as we are and we can fall in love with our own beauty, then we can love others without expectation or the need to change them.

Of course, looking after our body is something we can definitely improve many times over, but as we get older, the simpler things in life seem to serve us better.

For me, gone are the days of pushing my body to look a certain way and I am much more content to let things hang! I am growing into an elder and one that is able to say, 'I am not going to compete or create comparisons. I am not going to try to fit into society's norm. I will be who I am without the trimmings and fluff.'

Our bodies are supposed to change. The shape, the contours, the skin, the hair. It is what shows our eldership. We are always aging and it's fascinating! Look at the skin, it has done an amazing job for us. A time comes when we must give it a rest, let it slow down! And look at the gorgeous ripples and waves as the tide comes into shore.

The anti-aging business is hugely profitable and preys on women like me, reaching our sixties and being made to feel that we have no value. I've learnt these aging parts of me are important. I take them seriously, acknowledge what they teach me and know that this is what eldership is about. True eldership that says:

'We come with a wealth of experience and we have a voice to share.'

We can be that much needed example for younger men and women. For this is the journey, to embrace our own innocence, discover what is ours to do and bring that to sovereignty, supported by our own Wise Elder. If we cannot inhabit our Elder, then we cannot support the innocence that is yet to come, the children of the future.

Better to embrace the eldership archetype, standing strongly with staff in hand connecting it to the earth and the heavens, knowing we are a conduit for that hollow bone state. To inhabit ourselves fully and speak with wisdom in our hearts, with the life experience that is only ours to share that has brought us here to this place in our lives.

Elderhood & My Ancestors' Call

And sovereignty leads me to that world of eldership, a journey into the death of all things. It will bring me to my true nature and purpose and from here I learn to aspire to be the wisest elder I can be for the sake of my community. Without the Sacred Fool and the Wise Elder, my sovereignty is meaningless. I look back from this place to see what I have learned, what my experiences have been and what I bring forward from them.

It will of course be that I have failed many times. I will see clearly that all was not as I dreamt it would be and hold the bitter taste of some of my failings, yet still there is no complaint, because I have survived many tragedies along the way.

I will be only as I can be, I will do my very best to offer what I can and the meeting of Elder and Innocent will begin its journey.

* * *

In our modern societies and cultures, many people have seen indigenous nature and wisdom as being worthless. The hunter gatherers, the healers, the hedgerow gatherers, those connected to the land, as well as the artists, soul reclaimers and those on a non-religious spiritual path.

By forgetting to listen to our own ancestry and indigenous stories of our cultures and lands, we tend to ignore the harm that has been done. The harm is then repeated in today's societies and we do not learn from it. The stories fester in the silence, not known, not heard and not understood. There is no clarity and no healing. But they live through us in a way that creates negative energy in our civilisations, causing a lack of self esteem and a loss of spirituality and soul. Our communities have lost their soul, our environment has lost its soul and individuals have lost their soul. I believe that everything has a soul, even individual journeys and projects, professions and creative paths. This again is animism and the disbelief of it has contributed to the lack of spirituality, healthy principles and good living in our communities. It has affected leadership and left us in turmoil as to what is right and what is wrong. We barely know ourselves and our innate wisdom, not knowing who to believe. This has created such sickness on the planet that it is no wonder we are in trouble globally. Lost to the materialistic world we so easily admire, we are hungry for change, yet where do we look for it?

We have a dreaming body, a deeper sense of knowing. We can call on this dreaming body just as our ancestors did through sleeping, daydreaming, dancing, meditating and by being in nature. We can recall the indigenous roots of our own ancestors and find a reclaiming of our own soul and spiritual connection. We can, if we are willing, begin to reclaim animism, the beliefs of our ancestry and the spiritual understanding and healing of our soul journeys.

My own experience of this runs very deeply in a stream of consciousness that I write from at times and that I gather my information from.

Those in authority might frown upon our indigenous nature, where fear of its power is held in the roots of its own civilisation. Those who know themselves, of course, create fear in others, for those who know themselves are so much more empowered and do not need the voices of the ego driven elite.

That fear still festers in the hearts and minds of those who cannot abide its presence. They know too well the power that 'knowing oneself' holds, in the freedom makers, the artists, the healers and the medicine people of the land. They know it is a threat to their carefully sculpted paradigm of control and grandiosity.

And here on this healing path, for ourselves and our cultures, we will reside, we who 'know ourselves' are not going away, our voice is slowly being heard a little more fully and we will dance that dance into our streets, into our halls, into the writings and songs that are beginning to be taken notice of. Those who begin to shine their own light and step into the person they know themselves to be will threaten the organisations that can no longer control those individuals. And yes, it may be hard as individuals to break away from such places because the hooks are dug deeply into the flesh, but in time if the soul is to inhabit the body fully, then they will break away. It will hurt until that wound has healed, until the voice returns and the poet remembers their own forgotten language.

This is where we begin to revisit the place where the wound of our own culture began. The place where we were silenced as a creative being, as a healer or as a medicine man or woman. It was at that time that the soul of that part of our humanity became lost; we were dampened down and soulless. We can visit these wounds, find their story, sing their songs, feel into the heart of what needs to be healed and do the work necessary.

Only by going back there and rediscovering the nature of the wounds, can we reclaim those parts that have been missing and bring our soul's calling back fully into our present life.

We then might find a way to integrate what we discover into our world, for we cannot live in the same way as our ancestors but we can heal the old hurt so we ourselves can be free of it.

I have visited a few cultures where the old ways are still very much remembered, sometimes a little forgotten, but there is a trace of them and some traditions that are upheld. I found myself attracted to them; curious about them and in my fascination I tried to learn as much as possible. But one thing that I recognised was a need to honour and remember my own lineage first, to not forget that it exists.

Attraction to other cultures may suffice for a while, but eventually we need to come home to our own.

I often wished to learn something from other cultures, not to necessarily use it in my own culture, but to get a feel for it within the ancestry of the human race. We are all connected, of this I am sure, through the blood and the bones of our lineage that is undoubtedly connected down that long line of people. So I work with my own lineages, crafts and medicine and then I appreciate the crafts and medicine of others and what they carry.

In Namibia when we visited and danced with the San people and their extraordinary and simple way of life, I witnessed the deep presence of being with the earth that I have not experienced anywhere else. These simple, playful, innocent people truly inspire me and remind me of a part of myself. A part that often forgets to remain simple with my actions, forgets my connection to community, to the ground and to the elements. Despite living simply they are also quite complex, particularly in their histories and this shows significantly in their dances, the sounds of intricately precise polyphonic song and the rhythmic clapping that goes with it. Learning from the dancing doctors was a calling that inspired me to follow and find a deeper understanding, in order to reach something of my own healing and that of the potential of the dancing human race. Immersing myself in the few dances I experienced with them, something was touched on a cellular level that set off a much deeper understanding of what ecstatic dance was truly about.

What can we learn about our own dance from indigenous people?

These questions circulate occasionally in my thoughts, but mainly I learn from the experience of simply returning there in my mind, to the African landscape; drinking in the atmosphere, learning songs and experiencing the dances.

Many years ago, after a training I had completed in the UK, the group I was with exchanged presents, which were randomly given to each other. The gifts that were given to me were a picture of an African boy with a monkey and a model of an African elephant. I remember being completely baffled as to why I would receive them; they seemed very unlikely gifts for me. But taking them home I let them sit on my shelf and pondered on them. It wasn't until years later in a conversation out in the village of //xa //uba, North East Namibia, in the area of Tsumkwe, that I suddenly remembered the elephant I had been given, and it became clear... I remembered the gift just as we were talking about the Elephant Dance, which is a dance that the San dancing doctors hold ceremony with. I had been particularly drawn to this dance, more than the other dances and was clearly finding the power of it in my body. I remembered again my first dance with this and clearly getting the 'push and pull' between my own dance and that of the Elephant dance. Gradually, I found my way and the dancing doctors helped me to find a meeting place for the two medicine dances inside my body. From that time I was able to dance more with this mandorla, these medicine dances, and got to understand how my own dance was so deeply connected to the indigenous dance, the very first medicine dance of the human race.

Still, in my own offerings it had to be my particular dance, the one that held my own story, the one that was my offering to others. It could be influenced by my experiences of other cultures, but not rooted in them specifically, while knowing collectively that we are all rooted in that same one dance. The dance of trance or the dance to explore altered states, spirit guides and Num energy that the San people speak of is the biggest part of my experience as a dancer, connecting to the great mystery of the dancing human body.

Ecstatic dance is a healer, the way of spirit in movement.

As I become that dancing poetic elder myself, I keep taking steps along that creative path.

I breathe the nectar from the flourishing that aligns my own garden
and I remind myself of my true purpose, my sacred contract and the path that is mine to walk along.

Notes

Major Arcana

In the makeup of the Wheel, there are three main archetypal groups that hold a selection of particular archetypal qualities. The Hunter and Gatherer, which seek out what lies in the shadows, the old stories and what has been left unturned that must now be brought to the light.

They gather the information, bringing it to the Warrior who holds his or her stories as Allies, knowing that each one is part of the soul's journey and plays an important role within it, seeking information and wisdom from them, as they lay the foundations for the jewel that is hidden. The treasure and wisdom that our own stories hold, that we must seek and uncover.

The relationship between the two then takes on board the need to grow and to change. The Warrior is not afraid to do his or her work, to unravel and create that tapestry of new life, without hiding or staying silent. She/he knows all of those life-experiences as Allies and the greatest of teachings in this lifetime. Dancing his or her way through every challenge that is met, within and externally, seeking those awakening moments when the vibration and the quickening happens.

The Priestess and Magician represent aspects of the feminine and the masculine, the receptive and the active, overseeing the magic of this soul-work, giving it a whole new meaning to our life. The Magician plans and prepares, organising the chaos with the means of magic, keeping the balance and control, which at times is so necessary.

The Priestess listens and receives, awaiting the moment that only God can decide on. This one knows chaos all too well and knows that right at its centre there is creativity, which is what is needed if we are to change. Together they keep a balance of the rational and the subliminal.

They look together over our own Elder and our Sovereign, bringing tools and resources along the way, to keep the soul engaged and in service to the dream of the Innocent.

Our connection to God/Spirit will preside over all of this, making us aware of any flaws and failings, of decisions too quickly taken. And if we can, we learn to pay attention to every small detail, not allowing our own way of thinking to run away with us.

The spirits of our ancestors look over us, curious about how our journeys unfold and we are blessed.

Each stage gives us a sacred task to complete to find our way through the journey of soul's retrieval; The Wheel Of Soul's Return. None of it is necessarily easy, we may miss vital teachings and opportunities if it were. Without the ease, we are stretched just enough in order to grow. Sometimes we are buffeted into a corner of self doubt, where we can be fortunate enough to be on that pinnacle of falling apart and we can reach out and ask for help and guidance because we dare not take another step in any direction, knowing we will fall too deeply into our melancholic nature and possibly not return for many days!

* * *

At the root of my life there is an undying fear – the fear of life itself, of not being seen for who I am, of being alone. The fear and dread that is my constant companion simply because I am a human.

If not cared for, the fear leads to anxiety in every waking moment and permeates the very flesh of my bones. Yet it cannot stop me or hold me to the path of suffering and onward I must walk.

And in the creation of what I have discovered and come to trust, I have created this map. One that others, people like you, might find a useful tool to support your own journeys through fear, and through the minefield of doubts, addictions and dread. Through the misgivings, control and manipulation of others. We must find what is ours and ride the waves of its becoming. And at the same time, we must look at our own failings. We must acknowledge that we have not always been right and undo some of the harm done, harm that has kept us in a self-centred or self-obsessed world and not in the world of Spirit or God, where all is equal and all is connected and where we are not alone.

We have our wounds to bear and those wounds will have led us to dysfunctional patterns and habits. But all is not lost because we can be brave enough to look them in the eye and drop the mask of each one of them. We can bring ourselves back to the pure heart, the kindness of spirit and the willingness to be that better person we were born to be.

My Own Offering, the Mandorla

What became my own particular offering, when I looked back upon my life story, through the eyes of the Wheel? With the Seer at the centre and the support of the archetypal energies of the Wheel? I began to see what my own path was, the golden thread that ran through it and how all of my experiences had merged with one another quite clearly and so there it was... I found the body of work that was truly mine, now called the Magic Of Mandorla and the Rites of Passage that I would hold for others, the ceremonies and the attendance at births and deaths. The world of polarity, duality and the whole spectrum of life in between.

The question 'What is mine to do?', had found its answer. And this, what lay before my eyes, had been the process that I had followed, the discovery channels that awakened me to find out.

My story had found its way back from the original and sacred contract, my life carefully planned out to remind me of this and to gather wisdom along the way that would serve me, and others. So my offering to life was sculpted back into place and I could begin fully to give that offering to the world.

Would it be received? That was actually none of my business for it was up to others and what they themselves would make of it.

* * *

So what is this Mandorla?

At the centre of our Wheel sits the Mandorla within its own creativity and light. It is where we begin this work, finding its territory and landscape. It begins to show to us what work needs to be done and where we need more faith.

It is a way to literally see ourselves, in the light of a divine witness, within the power of potential, and to illuminate the shadows that are not always obvious. We learn to witness our own myth and life story, how we behave and some of the shadowy aspects of character or characteristics that get caught up in daily living that do not serve us. These are ours to address and we ourselves must find new ways to deal with them. Once they are seen and witnessed, there is no going back and our own Seer's potential can begin to vision in a future that unveils the possibilities of our new way of living.

A life with true meaning is a life that does not depend on the 'role' that society has labelled us with, or that we have 'seemingly' chosen. We will all arrive at a time in our lives where we must accept that life has much more importance than that and we cannot stay the same. For that will be a life wasted on frivolous human endeavour and will create a life of hurt, that lays victim to our egoism, our thinking mind and thoughts that no longer serve us. We remain a victim to our childhood or adolescence and there is so much more opportunity than that to be explored. The myth is being made known and its shadow energy lessened, we become who we need to be and we know what is ours to do with it.

Let us ask the questions 'Who are we at the very core and centre of our being? What is our purpose and how do we find it?'

As human beings, we can exist on multiple planes of being. The one that we are usually most aware of, however, is the material world. By its nature, the material world is a place of duality – a place of opposites that we often experience as being in conflict with one another. Examples include heaven and earth, light and dark, masculine and feminine, loyalty and betrayal, to name a few. The polarity between these opposites creates a fundamental tension from the beginning of its time, that has the potential to be either profoundly destructive or powerfully generative and creative. The evidence of the destructive consequences of this tension lies all around us in the terrible scourges of war, inequality and conflict within and between individuals, groups and societies.

The key to transforming these destructive consequences of conflict into life-affirming outcomes lies in how we relate to the tension between the opposites. When we can hold the tension within ourselves, bearing the pain, beauty and terror that this brings, we bring the two opposing elements together, creating a space in which the split between the two can be resolved.

This space in traditional work with conflict is called the 'mandorla' – a word derived from 'almond' in Italian, which refers to the almond shape created when two circles overlap. The mandorla, also known as the vesica piscis, is the sacred space of our soul work. When we stand in this place, we have the ability to transform what was once a curse into powerful medicine for the soul.

In my work, I simply think of that place in the middle. The place where polarities meet, where we stand in the tension between those opposites and the vibration is felt. It is the great orgasm of life, this union that has been known to us as a creative force, where all of life began and we feel at this time more deeply than at any other time in our lives!

This is a place that awakens the Seer and we begin to follow the journey of soul retrieval with a keen eye, observing every moment with an awakened heart. We enter the gathering time of our lives and become the hunter and gatherer of our own truth.

It is from this place that deep change can begin to happen. It might rock us, it might shake us, but it is our job to stay rooted, to stand strong and to welcome the turbulence as it works its magic upon us. Which is why I call it the Magic of the Mandorla.

So being a middle child, I knew a little of this place, being born on the solstice, a place between dark and light and from those moments and many other places in the 'middle landscape'. I became fascinated with this way of experiencing, which I now call 'Middle Earth Medicine Ways'.

This Mandorla territory exaggerates for us the power of that central force – where we are stretched beyond our normal existence and yet is part of who we are. The magic of all we can become when we are brave enough to *be* that meeting of opposing forces within us. It exists and we cannot escape it. I have discovered it time and time again, struggled with it, resisted it and pushed it aside. But it always comes back, either biting me on the backside, or seducing me into its lull of familiarity.

For it is the essence of who we are and we cannot fight it.

Does this sound in any way familiar to you? Or is it completely alien? Personally, I feel absolutely sure that we have all felt the pain and profundity of the 'power of polarities' within us. We may choose to call it the power of opposites, wherever it exists at any point in our lives. We may have ignored or denied it, or tried to enforce its retreat by insisting on our own self-will to be the deciding factor, rather then leave it to the magic to inform us.

Can we trust it?

And when we do become aware of it, or feel it, how do we react to it? I began to create a particular piece of work, one I called The Magic Of Mandorla, which is a dance of acceptance, to stand in the centre of two circles of energy that are overlapping, creating tension in that central place. This represents a tension that births a light, a power place of illumination. It represents the true essence of the soul, the power and the humility that bares us to the bone – that tears our heart to shreds yet reboots it to a greater strength.

Dancing with the mandorla is a stance for freedom, for the Seer needs to awaken within us and exist deeply in connection with our purpose, and it has no doubts about our truth. It might shake us as we dance in its wave, it may frighten us when we shed these old skins that enforce a structure too old to be taken seriously any more. And it might shine the greatest light from our core, into a world where there is no escape but to be seen.

The reality is, we have seen it!

Taking the mandorla into our journey, into our heart, creating a totally new awareness of who we are is a brave step to take. It's a creative one too, for I believe we cannot grow without creativity. It is our birthright, no matter who we are. For we are creative beings in all of our magnificence.

The soul calls for creativity, to help it to arrive more fully in the bones of the body. Without it the soul becomes lost, meaningless and soullessness ensues.

We are blessed to have both sides of the mandorla's circles, to have both sides of the coin. Even though the tension felt between these opposites can be extreme and we can lean towards over protection and too much control, protecting our hearts from pain or fear. But once we can move those elements out of the way, then energy can flow more easily and the magic of the mandorla can reveal itself to us.

Can we bear the tension?

It cannot be borne by the mind but must be felt via the body. The thinking mind will keep us fixated on the problem, but the body and movement will help us to release and find what is really the truth, the absolute truth.

If you are called to dance with the mandorla's energy and discover your potential from the deepest part of your inner being, then you are being asked to bear your soul, to open yourself to who you really are and this my dear friend, is no easy task. But I can promise you, stand in that place long enough and you will indeed be witness to your own light!

Sometimes within our individual self and within the self of our worn-out society, there is no answer to conflict. There is, however, a way to stand within the centre of the opposing forces. Conflict creates tremendous energy. If we leave out judgment, then that 'energy' can become a vibration of light. Not always just a single light but many lights, sending out a vibration that is LOVE!

Notes

Soul & Ego

And so with our Sovereign, our Sacred Fool and our Wise Elder embodied, we can make that offering that is ours to make. Learning, with the guidance of these three, how to bring the soul and ego into one sacred union, which is at the core of the most authentic vocations.

There is a difference between what we have as our gifts and how we then offer that to our community or society. We have our gifts and we have our delivery system. These are two very different things and we need to become aware of them both.

One is connected more deeply to our soul; the other is connected to our ego. Our soul holds the gifts; rooted in the depths of our psyche, discovered when we visit our wounds, our creativity, the stories of our childhood and the depths of our inner eco-identity, the poet within and all we have learned along the way; the journey so far.

The delivery system is what we learn from our engagement with family, society and communities. Our ego has learnt how to be in the world, how to manage the immediate world. Sometimes in good ways that serve and sometimes in ways that do not. But it is all learning.

Some may have a strong sense of how to deliver something. We may learn a technique, a form. We may be good at speaking and have much knowledge to impart, or we may know how to sell and market really well. We may be a teacher in a school or college and all of this can work well in our delivery. But if we do not know the true gift that we carry, our own life's work, then we are missing the true purpose of what our delivery needs to be. It is not complete without its soul purpose.

We may have a vocation and we may have a job. Which is which?

Discovering our vocation gives us a strong feeling of suitability for a particular occupation, calling, life's work, mission or purpose. Our job is how we earn a living. These can be two different things. One comes from the need to survive, the other comes from the need to give back and to fulfil our lives.

The daytime job is part of the support for our vocation but not always the vocation itself.

My teacher once said, as I learnt to offer the dance, 'Don't give up your day job!' It would have been too soon to put everything into my vocation and there would not have been enough money to survive. So it is a timely thing. We are not necessarily here to earn a wage from our vocation and only time will tell if we are meant to, when the time is right, if ever at all.

So it is important to understand how our delivery system supports our soul's purpose. If we do not have a delivery system, then we can become lost, remaining unknown to others and our work only a way of self-gratification. Our task is to explore our offerings and gifts from the world of soul and to engage with the ego in a harmonious way. Our ego begins to know what it is good at and supports the soul to become embodied and to step out into the world.

If the ego is healthy and knows to remain humble to the calling of the soul, and is always reminded of the core wound it has lived through, then it will do well in the making of its path, to serve others with similar wounds. And this healthy ego will know how to express the empathy needed, to be authentic and integral to its cause. If the ego is unhealthy, then chances are that purpose will not be fulfilled in the way that it needs to be.

Together the soul and the ego can form a healthy allegiance and a way of being within the world that is both right-sized, humble and authentic.

We all have a mythological and poetic identity, something we are born with that develops as we age. But also as we grow older it can become lost, as we create our social identity.

Social identity is really important to help us establish ourselves. We develop our own ego characteristics that will help us to engage more with the world. Without the ego we are not able to form relationships, make decisions, create our careers or educate ourselves, amongst many other things known to the human race.

Social identity can also be created from our survival mechanisms. What habits have we developed in order to survive? Without these survival mechanisms, we would more than likely have suffered too greatly and would have been unable to live under the conditions laid out for us. We will need to review many of these habits and actions and learn at some point how to change them. They do not necessarily support the soul to live an embodied life filled with purpose.

We are born to play a unique role on earth. We have a destiny, a role, a quality to offer our communities. We have no idea what it is at first, no language to create it with. There needs to be a process that will help us to remember what that role is.

This often appears to us as a metaphor from beyond the human world. We can experience many revelations. We may just hear a story or see a particular character that stirs something within us, or attracts us. It may be a place we visit that moves us beyond all reason. This 'resonating with the other' can seem like a blessing, but it can also seem like a curse.

Who knows where it will take us, discomfort and excitement is often felt together.

So we might immerse ourselves into the sludge of life, meeting the edges of our familiar and safe existence or we might open to the quickening, that fires up the creative life force in us and allows us to be curious about turning every corner, knowing there is adventure ahead.

I am aware of my own creativity, my poetry and my writings, my dance and my offerings from the dreamtime. It has taken me many years to really value what these are, as the truth of my own identity and to understand how it can serve others as well as the earth. This I now know to be my vocation and purpose.

Is there a song calling to us, a mystery song that wakes us in the night, that beckons in our dreams, that as we walk down country lanes or stroll past rivers, suddenly finds its voice through our lips? Does an unusual situation take us by the hand and show us a different side of life, even if it is way out of our comfort zone? Can we allow the intrigue to take hold of us and enter in with fascination at our side?

Whatever it is, it invites the beloved to dance more fully into our world, a melody that dances through us with a longing to participate more fully.

Are we willing to surrender to that song?

If we give it voice it may mean that we are saying 'yes' to the mystery that is unfolding. We may find ourselves at a crossroads, wondering which way to turn. But there is no right or wrong way. Once we hear that calling we cannot go the wrong way, unless we shrink in fear and hide ourselves back into a mediocre life, where we feel safe and secure but with nothing to inspire us, with nothing to offer, and certainly no gratitude for the life that has been given to us. Or we go on that journey with heaviness, complaining about every moment, no curiosity about what it might be teaching us.

Is there a quickening in your body? Do you feel nervous as the trembling begins?

Well then, that is good. Let yourself feel it, because it will guide you well. Let it vibrate your very being, shaking the core of who you think you are. Go into it; ask it to show you the song, the dance, the emerging force of your poetic nature.

Then listen deeply, one step at a time, into the dark, into the Cave of Intelligence. Fill the space around you with poems, with dances. Write letters, make gestures, feel your emotions and pay attention to memories, and write down your dreams. With every meeting of the ordinary and the not so ordinary, with people, and places, be grateful and embrace with an open heart. What can I learn from this person, from how fascinating he or she is?

Let the grief break from your belly, meet with the mad woman or the mad man in your psyche and sharpen your claws.

Here we destabilise ourselves and this is good. Ecstasy, fear, anger, a sense of feeling unbalanced, this all enables us to go deeper into the mystery. It takes us to the lower worlds, where there is so much more to explore and where it is so necessary for us to go if we are to connect with the soul. This is where the soul and the ego begin to meet. They need each other; they need to fall in love.

The soul is the dreamer, the one that lives within the mystery, that is seeking its mythological story and bringing it into the world. Manifesting it through the creativity and the story line of its life . The ego becomes the hands of the soul as it falls deeper and deeper into this connection. Without the ego, the soul has no hands. It is, therefore, not able to manifest the myth into the world where the soul and ego support each other towards true growth. Ego without soul has no journey to go on, it simply creates for the sake of personal possession, for self-gratification.

There is no sense of owning one's archetype, of being in service to others or community and most certainly not to the world.

Until the ego meets with the soul, true love cannot be born.

I pray we can change attitudes to how we live on the earth and how we respect her beauty and what she offers to us. I feel the celebration of what has been in our bones for many life times; the art of dance, the creativity of theatre and the deeply satisfying connections that community brings. I pray we can find healthy ways to lessen the grip of trauma and neglect and free our hearts and emotions in that one beautiful dance of creativity.

I pray that every time I make a new acquaintance or experience something new in my life, that I can feel the possibility of growing part of myself, of accepting that new experience as a possibility of growing up, maturing into the person I need to be. If I am to fully do God's work, then I need to be open to where I am put and guided to in any given moment. It might not be the most profound experience, it could be something quite mundane, but if I go into it with a curious heart, then I cannot help but gain and learn from it.

* * *

And now to follow on in my own journey and offer that outwards. I support you in mapping out your journey, to find the key moments and the gateways that help you to identify what is yours to do as a pioneer, a creative of your art and healing; to explore your own soul, to be willing to embrace those ecstatic awakenings, to prepare for their timely event.

If you find this book useful then you can use it as a guide alongside the dances and explorations of Middle Earth Medicine, which supports you to awaken through movement, dance, meditation, creativity and sharing with others. Already there are people guiding and serving others with these ways and we welcome you on board to share your story with us and return to the path and journey of your soul.

* * *

And so, in order to follow my creative style, to take my understanding of the Wheel even further, I needed to make something with imagery that would further serve and maybe even delight others on this sacred and creative path. So I offer images alongside this book, paintings created by my dear mother-in-law, Brenda May. At the inspiring age of 85, she took her art onto the canvas and began to take my words and ideas, weaving her magic, to create as only an artisan can, the offering that will be yours. There to inspire you, to help you awaken a part of yourself, an inner part that can interpret experiences in many different ways with different meanings, that does not simply rely on one way. We introduce The Middle Earth Oracle Cards.

The book that accompanies the Oracle Cards is filled with the images, explanations, poetry and prose with explanations of each card.

You are invited to explore with the cards, to use them to help you witness your own journey and to support you to find the creative aspects of your own soul-searching and purpose.

Continue this thought provoking journey with this Oracle of cards, allowing them to be your companions.

Notes

And The Journey Complete

Our meeting with the death of all things is the deepest surrender. If we have lived our lives well and shared our experiences with others, then it will surely be our greatest teaching and offering.

The soul's journey this lifetime is complete. We have done our work well. We know our own myth and we know the archetypal character that we hold and one that has discovered its purpose and has embodied it.

We can now rest, knowing that others will follow in our footsteps and whatever we brought to the world now has its own journey.

How might we let go, give up this one life and befriend that greatest teacher, facing it with fear that is not without courage?

For there is no courage without fear.

We return to the mystery, to that ultimate connection with our higher power and we begin to dream again...

Notes

Apprenticeship

Embodying our purpose and true identity.

I invite you to journey with me into the depths of your own heart, into the profundity of your own life experience and to dance yourself free of limitations by exploring archetypes, life stages, tools and a host of resources, letting go of limiting beliefs about yourself and accessing a greater wisdom that is your birthright. Together we can conjure the necessary requirements for personal empowerment, so you can become your own Sovereign.

The Sovereign, that is the particular archetype you were born to be, that knows its soul's purpose.

We use meditations in movement, ecstatic dance, ritual-theater, creativity and community sharing, plus a range of themes that empower the soul.

Whether you wish to deepen your understanding of your own purpose and skills, or whether you would like to share movement/dance sessions or shamanic processes or one to one work with others, then working with this Medicine Wheel, may be the process that is right for you.

Together we learn to support ourselves and to support others in finding our greatest potential and our fullest purpose in life. This is both healing and liberating for everyone and especially empowering and healing for ourselves. It is here we learn about who we really are and what it is we are here to do.

We work together by apprenticing on workshops and gatherings and taking part in the sharing with the offering of Middle Earth Medicine and its teachings. You can join as us a student of this work, or take a deeper dive into apprenticeship.

* * *

The Gathering, a Deeper Knowing and The Offering

These are the Outer Realms of the work being done on a soul level when we engage in the inner 'work' segments of the Wheel. Our aim is to empower these major archetypal qualities in our lives; The Hunter-Gatherer, The Warrior-Ally and The Magician-Priestess and to use these to inform our myth, our poetic identity and our soul purpose.

The workshops we do reflect this:

- ✓ The Seer and Mandorla; the central space of our soul work. The power of polarity.
- ✓ The Story; minor arcana. The dwellings, the life stages, the archetypes, the resources and the tools.
- ✓ The Over-Seers; major arcana. Hunter-Gatherer, Warrior-Ally, Priestess-Magician

The minor arcana workshops are:

- ✓ 'Beyond The Veil'
- ✓ 'Reclaimed Innocence'
- ✓ 'Meeting The Wild'
- ✓ 'Heart Matters & The Cave Of Intelligence'
- ✓ 'The Oracle Of Medicine' & 'Finding our Spirit Song' (with medicine bag creation)

✓ 'The Body Oracle'

✓ 'The Circle, The Fire & The Phoenix'

The Over-Seers intensive workshops are:

✓ 'Oracle Of Dance' (Hunter-Gatherer; knowing our life story)

✓ 'The Fabric Of My Soul' (Warrior & Ally; creating and manifesting)

✓ 'Magic Of Mandorla Intensive' (Magician & Priestess; becoming our offering); discovering the polarity of soul and ego; the core wound and the aspiration.

✓ Apprenticeship – working alongside Caroline

✓ Inauguration Ceremony – Your archetype and purpose made known

✓ 'Hunting & The Vision Walk' – Passing It On

For more information on apprenticing
the soul's journey with Caroline and her other work,
please visit this website:

www.middleearthmedicine.com

We cannot know the truth about ourselves
by only using our mind… so go on a deeper search
in the depths of your own caverns and
find out who you really are.

Go deeper because you always can, knowing
that the gift that YOU are,
lies as a hidden jewel deep inside you.

Never give up, keep asking those questions and
meeting the place of profundity,
where the two worlds meet.

Asking yourself – '*Who am I?*'

For you are the light,
hiding in your own darkness!

Printed in Great Britain
by Amazon

66793706R00135